Then the End Will Come

Jim Montgomery

Great News about the Great Commission

William Carey Library
PASADENA, CALIFORNIA

Dawn Ministries
7899 Lexington Drive, Suite #200-B
Colorado Springs, CO 80920
Phone: (719) 548-7460
Fax: (719) 548-7475
Compuserve address: 71102,2745

Published by
WILLIAM CAREY LIBRARY
P. O. Box 40129
Pasadena, CA 91114
Phone (818) 798-0819

Library of Congress Cataloging-in-Publication Data

Montgomery, James H., 1930-
Then the end will come! / Jim Montgomery
p. cm.
Includes bibliographical references.
ISBN 0-87808-272-7 (alk. paper)
1. Missions. 2. Home missions. I. Title.
BV2061.M66 1997
266--dc21 96-49863
CIP

Cover design by David Thomason

Printed in the United States of America

Dedication

To the "John Knoxers" who embody the cry "Give me my country or I die"; to the intercessors, the denomination and para-church heads and the host of local pastors and laymen who have caught the vision and committed their lives to see their nations "filled with the knowledge of the glory of the Lord"; to the hundreds and thousands of such men and women who, in my mind, represent a continuing list of names to be added to the heroes of the faith mentioned in Hebrews 11; to them I humbly and gratefully dedicate this book.

"Make known among the nations
what he has done."
Psalm 105:1

Contents

Preface

In the Fall of 1974, Church and mission leaders in the Philippines committed themselves to a vision and a project that, if successful, would greatly speed the discipling of their nation and provide a dynamic model for completing the Great Commission for the whole world in our time.

Both have been realized.

Their dream was to see a vibrant evangelical church planted in every rural village and city neighborhood and at least one for every 1,000 Filipinos of every class, kind and condition by the year 2000. This called for a ten-fold increase in their number of congregations from about 5,000 to 50,000 in 26 years.

Just over 20 years later, they are ahead of schedule. Instead of the 14,500 churches they would now have, had they continued growing at their previous rate, there are actually over 38,000. This additional 23,500 congregations also means about 2.35 million more Filipinos have come to know the Lord *and become active, growing, witnessing members in local churches* than otherwise would have been the case.

Sure enough, the Church of the rest of the world has taken note. Currently, there are over 100 such projects under way covering more than 85 percent of the world's population. In 30 of these DAWN—Discipling A Whole Nation—projects, national Churches are effectively working at planting a targeted 3 million new congregations! Soon the other 70 will hold national congresses where they will set goals and implement plans for the number of new congregations they feel the Lord calling them to establish.

By working at "filling the earth with the knowledge of the glory of the Lord"[1] with the incarnate Christ visible in local congregations within easy access of every person in every people group and nation in the world, these national Churches are implementing the strategy for the end of the age, the mission that will most directly lead to the completion of the Great Commission and usher in the return of the Lord.

The full story of the nature and development of the DAWN approach is told in *DAWN 2000: 7 Million Churches to Go*.[2] The book you hold in your hand, however, tells the stories of those national Churches and national leaders who have shouldered the burden for the discipling of their nations and some of the incredible results the Lord of the harvest is bringing about as a result of their efforts.

---

[1] Hab. 2:14, Num. 14:21, Is. 11:9, Ps. 72:19.
[2] Jim Montgomery, *DAWN 2000: 7 Million Churches to Go* (Pasadena, CA: William Carey Library, 1989). Available from Dawn Ministries, 7899 Lexington Dr., Colorado Springs, CO 80920, (719) 548-7460; or from William Carey Library, P.O. Box 40129, Pasadena, CA 91114, (818) 798-0819.

Introduction

Bridging the gap from 1989 to 1996

While attending a gathering of pastors and evangelical leaders in Zimbabwe in 1990, I gave a copy of my just-released *book, DAWN 2000: 7 Million Churches To Go,* to Ngwiza Mnkandla. The next morning he said to me in surprisingly colloquial English, "Jim, you dirty guy, you kept me awake all night. Once I started reading your book, I couldn't stop."

Now I knew this was no page turner, no action-packed mystery thriller that held you spellbound until you found out how the hero emerged triumphant over his wicked and ingenious enemies. So what was the compulsion?

"This is exactly the strategy God put on my heart when I was a barefoot sheepherder in my native village," he said. "This is what we must do to win Zimbabwe for Christ."

I am truly astonished at the number of times I have heard if not these exact words at least the exact sentiment expressed by leaders from Afghanistan to Zimbabwe.

Yet, in Dawn Ministries, we do very little to "sell" the Discipling A Whole Nation (DAWN) concept. Our six regional coordinators are spread so thin as to be responsible each for 10 or 12 huge nations or up to 50 or more countries of various sizes. We have no missionary teams residing in a country to support a project. We give away virtually no money. For an international organization, our mailing list is minuscule. Without any effort or financing on our part, the *DAWN 2000* book has been translated currently into 10 languages in such standards as French and Spanish and in such exotic languages as Russian and Arabic. These four alone are spoken by over a billion people.

Still, DAWN leaps borders and continents and multiplies seemingly of its own energy. How to explain all this?

C. Peter Wagner, my friend and mentor and one of the top missiologists of our day, gave his answer after reading *DAWN 2000* while still in manuscript form.

"You've made your point," he said to me. "You have demonstrated that seven million more churches is about the right number, that planting them in all the right places is the most direct way to complete the Great Commission and that the DAWN strategy is the vehicle to get us there."

Lois LeBar amplified on this a bit. "Dr. Lois" is one of the professors I respected most in my Wheaton College and graduate school days. She made a greater impact on my life and ministry and hence on the DAWN strategy than any other teacher. Though now 87 and quite deaf, her mind is as bright and sharp as ever. After I recently sent her a copy of *DAWN 2000: 7 Million Churches To Go*, she shot back the following:

"I am praying for all the efforts made for the year 2000, but all the strategies have been overwhelming until I read what you suggest from Scripture.

"You've broken down the formidable task into feasible steps. It all seems so workable and sensible. And so balanced! The vision and the implementation. The Lord doing what only he can do, and man shouldering his responsibility. An urgency, yet enough case studies to show that it can be done. Statistical data to guarantee credibility, and yet the book is readable."

Comments like these, which are representative of uncounted similar statements from leaders all over the world, tend to affirm what I had already come to believe: that the DAWN strategy comes from the heart of God, that it is based on solid biblical and missiological principles, that the churches and nations of the world are ripe for such an approach and even that this is a primary strategy for the completion of the Great Commission and the end of the age.

Though this book is written as a sequel to *DAWN 2000: 7 Million Churches to Go*, it is complete in itself. For a fuller history and explanation of the DAWN strategy, however, the reader will find it useful to refer to that book as well.

While it is unlikely that the seven million new churches I spoke of in the last book will all be planted by the end of AD 2000, I feel no sense of disappointment. AD 2000 is a significant milestone in the history of the Church, but it is no magic date. The Lord does things on his own schedule.

If anything, my faith and boldness have greatly increased. What has happened since 1989 when the last book was published is remarkable. Furthermore, our sense from the Lord in Dawn Ministries is that we are really just at the bottom of the curve, that exponential growth of the Church in nation after nation will be the rule in the days immediately ahead and that the vast number of unreached people groups will be entered and the process of filling them with vibrant congregations will be heading toward completion.

For as I look at what is happening in the Church and in the world, I feel the prophetic word welling up within me that the consummation of the age is at hand. It is within our grasp to actually complete the Great Commission and thereby pave the way for the return of the Lord.

That's what *Then the End Will Come* is all about.

Jim Montgomery
September, 1996

Part I

The Earth Shall be Filled

Chapter One

The Time of the End

'Go your way, Daniel, because the words are closed up and sealed until the time of the end.'

Daniel 12:9

Growing up in San Jose, California, I had a friend whose father, a Baptist minister, spent 20 years studying every Bible prophecy that spoke of events to come. He used the year-for-a-day method, the only approach he found consistent with biblical teaching. That is, for example, the "70 weeks" in the Daniel prophecy[1] would consist of 70 weeks times seven days or a total of 490 "days." Assigning one year for each day would therefore give us 490 years. Using this approach, he delved into history to see what transpired at each projected milestone for each of the "days" or years mentioned in Old Testament prophecies.

He did this each for what astronomers call the solar year—its length measured by the sun—, the lunar year—its length measured by the moon—and the conjoint movements of both orbs called the calendar year.

"God uses all of these years in the Bible," Harold E. Barton wrote in 1962.[2] "The difference between them is great over a long period of time. Thus God has veiled the fulfillment of chronological prophecies from past generations."

In the book that resulted from his passionate search—*It's Here: The Time of the End*—he concluded that no matter how you look at it, there is no date mentioned in the Bible beyond the year 2009.

Plainly, he did *not* say the Lord would return that year, or that the Lord could not return before then or even after. He simply made the observation that no matter how he projected the time line of various prophecies using the three different measurements for the length of a year, he could not extend it beyond AD 2009.

Now, more than three decades later, what this relatively obscure minister was saying in a corner is being shouted from the housetops by many evangelical leaders. In like manner, none of them is pointing to a particular year for the Lord's return, but they are all recognizing we are in the end times.

During a period of two weeks while writing this book, for example, four different unsolicited books on world revival crossed my desk. One of them referred to four other recent books on the subject, and somebody else told me about Bill Bright's new book on revival. Since then I have repeatedly come across books, articles, seminars and messages on the theme of world revival and the end of the age.

Practically with one voice these respected evangelical authors whose books I read were saying that world revival was on the way if not already here, that this would probably be the last and greatest revival ever to hit the world and that it would result in "...the most productive period of evangelism in history."[3] It would see whole nations being reached, the completion of the Great Commission and would lead to the return of the Lord Jesus Christ.

The revival/evangelism connection

These authors are in general agreement that revival and "productive evangelism" go hand in hand. This reminds me of the conclusion Southern Baptist missionary James Slack came to after studying the growth of the Church in the Philippines in the 1970's.

"If church growth is one strong indication of revival," he said, "then what is happening in the Philippines must be the longest revival ever."[4]

Twenty years later, I find myself in considerable agreement with Slack. If church growth is one strong indication of revival, then what is happening not only in the Philippines but in many other parts of the world indicates we are in a revival of global proportions.

As I write this, for example, a report from Berna Salcedo, our Dawn Ministries Regional Coordinator for Latin America, has hit my desk. In his just-completed trip to Peru he found that careful research had shown the Church as a whole planting new churches at an incredible Average Annual Growth Rate (AAGR) of 15 percent for the three years prior to their first *Amanecer* (Spanish for "dawn") Congress in 1993.

To put this in perspective, if the Church of the whole world were to grow at this rate from 1994 to the end of the millennium, we would reach 13 million Bible-oriented congregations or one for every 460 people on the globe!

All of this to say that 15 percent AAGR is *very* significant. Salcedo also found, incidentally, that in the first year *after* the 1993 DAWN-type Congress, the Church had increased its church-planting rate by almost 50 percent, up to an annual growth rate of about 21 percent! As we will see throughout the book, this is just one small example of what is happening in many places around the world.

My experience is that few Christians, particularly in America, are aware of such growth. A fourth-generation missionary to Asia that you will read about later in the book, for example, says that this is the day of the Holy Spirit in India. "It breaks my heart," he told a group of us in a recent interview. "India is the best-kept missionary secret in the world. I met a veteran missionary to India the other day and she said, 'Why do you lie about what is going on? What you claim is impossible.'"

Still, it's not only possible but it's happening. India and China are a couple of the brightest examples, but it's happening in enough other regions to demonstrate an increasing world-wide phenomenon indicating that revival is already here or, at the very least, well on the way.

Not yet universal

It cannot be said, of course, that the Church is growing like this in even a majority of the nations of the world. As a case in point, a study by Southern Baptist researcher Stephen Whitten in 1993 showed that 57 denominations representing 61 percent of all Christian churches in the United States[5] had been increasing their number of congregations by an AAGR of just over *one tenth of one percent* between 1980 and 1992! The Church in Peru grew 210 times as fast in 1995!

The huge Southern Baptists themselves were at about .5 percent and even the prolific Assemblies of God were only up to 1.4 percent. The most significant growth of an evangelical denomination of any considerable size was the International Church of the Foursquare Gospel. They were increasing congregations at a 4 percent AAGR.

Around the world, growth rates vary, they go up and they go down. Traditionally-resistant Japan, for example, had maintained a sluggish 1.7 AAGR for church planting for the 30-year period from 1960 to 1990. Between 1990 and 1993, however, 64 denominations together doubled that rate to 3.6 percent, and 14 of these denominations grew at an astonishing—for Japan—10.27 percent AAGR![6]

By contrast, while Christians around the world marvel at the growth of the Church in Korea, their membership increase plummeted from 9 percent in 1989 to .6 percent in 1992 and actually declined by 4 percent in 1993![7] But as can be documented and to some extent will be shown in this book, there is enough rapid growth taking place in nations of the world to indicate that global revival is at hand.

Other indications of world revival

The mushrooming growth in the number of born-again believers in many nations and across some whole continents in recent decades, of course, is just one indicator of world revival. There is a bunch more. Look at the incredible proliferation of mega prayer movements, the increasing publication of books and articles on revival, the host of stories of God's direct revelation (including dreams, visions and prophetic utterances) and intervention in the lives of Hindus and Muslims among others, the mounting number of plans for world evangelization, the AD2000 and Beyond Movement, the new thrust of the World Evangelical Fellowship, the growing zeal to enter all the still-unreached people groups of the world, the evidences of the world-wide Body beginning to function as a body through an array of networks, and the startling growth of the two-thirds world missionary movements. These are all signs of revival on an unprecedented global scale.

On top of all this is simply the *need* for revival. As Robert E. Coleman writes in *The Coming World Revival,* "We need to remember that it is usually in periods of momentous crisis that great revivals are born. Our sense of helplessness, properly directed, actually can make us more sensitive to the need for supernatural grace."[8]

If all the media messages that are hurled at us, if the sermons we are hearing, if our own daily experience doesn't tell us we are in momentous crisis, then surely we are out of touch.

But we do not despair. As the prophet assures us, "When the enemy comes in like a flood, I (the Lord) will raise up a standard against him" (Is. 59:19 KJV). The good news is that our current world crisis can usher in a great revival leading to the evangelization of the world!

What if revival came?

I began to see more fully this connection between revival power and completing the Great Commission during our first term as missionaries in the Philippines. My research into the rapid growth of the Foursquare denomination in 1965, for example, led to the book *New Testament Fire in the Philippines.*[9] What attracted my attention to this denomination was a preliminary study that indicated it was growing at a rate five times as fast as the combined growth of 72 other denominations in the country.

After recording the testimonies of more than 200 of their converts, I had to conclude there was a great spiritual dynamic at work behind their rapid expansion. Visions, healings, miracles and testimonies of the experience of being filled with the Spirit were all part of dramatic conversions and vibrant numerical growth as well as growth in the Word and in the Lord. Here was a clear connection between revival power and the growth of the Church.

In the process of studying the Foursquare Church in the Philippines, I discovered the same kind of New Testament experience was producing tremendous growth in nations all over the world. Furthermore, it wasn't all happening just in Pentecostal circles.

The great Zulu revival

One such revival emerged in 1966 from the ministry of Erlo Stegen, a Dutch Reformed evangelist working among the Zulu in South Africa. If such a revival were to spread throughout the continent, the results would be almost beyond imagining. In a three-hour tape recording made in 1977, Stegen gave a detailed account of the movement that has continued up to this time. More recent on-site observers, including Dawn Ministries missionary Ted Olsen, verify the continuing presence of this movement of the Spirit.

In the 1950's, Stegen was a typical Dutch Reformed pastor and white Afrikaner who had enormous hurdles to overcome before the Lord could use him as a vessel for an incredible outpouring of the Spirit.

A first step was when his own pastor got converted, followed by Stegen's conversion and call to the ministry. This call, however, was definitely not as a missionary to the blacks. He confessed there was a time when he hated them. He would hit them, swear at them and otherwise illtreat them.

Then there was the hurdle of his feelings towards other Christians. He had nothing to do with them and even felt sorry for them. His Church was the right Church with the right teaching. They did not even have to be born again since they were christened as children.

Once these obstacles and many others were overcome and he actually began a ministry among the black Zulus, he wanted to see things literally happen as they did in the Bible. "We would hold campaigns for 6, 10, or 14 months non-stop," he testified. "But no fire came. We would start with up to 600 people, but after six months there would be 100 less. After a year there would perhaps be 200. If we came back after a couple of years we would find maybe 20 to 50 people meeting once a week for Bible study or prayer. We were going backwards."

After 12 years of massive but relatively fruitless ministry, a major crisis came in his life when a woman in simple faith asked if his God could heal her deranged, mad daughter. He took the daughter into his home and prayed for her for three weeks, but he had to take her back to the mother and admit defeat.

Now doubts began to form and modernism crept into his mind. He would decide what was true in the Bible and what was not. In desperation, he led his ministry team into a study of the book of Acts. The more they saw the actions of the early Church, the more their hearts broke.

Revival finally came on a Saturday when a great wave of conviction and repentance took place. "After 12 years of ministry," he said, "I felt disqualified. I saw myself (as if I were) in a heathen temple bowing down before strange gods. I cried out to God to come down or I'll die. I saw for the first time what it meant that God's Spirit was a *Holy* Spirit."

As the team later gathered, Stegen reports that God came down with a mighty rushing wind. The Spirit of God moved over the place where they were meeting and into nearby homes. People came out to see what was happening.

One of the first people to come from a distance was a witch who owned a school for training other witches. Stegen later learned she walked over five miles to get there. For 12 years, he had tried to convert witches, but to no avail. Now there was one coming to him.

"What would you like?" he asked her.

"I want Jesus to set me free," she replied.

Curious, he asked her who invited her, who preached to her.

"Nobody," she said. "If Jesus doesn't set me free today, I will die and go to hell. These are satanic bonds and chains by which I am bound."

Stegen relayed to her through an interpreter that she must confess her sins and then they would pray for her. When they commanded the devil to come out in the name of Jesus, there was a mocking reply. "We are 300 strong warriors," they said. "No one will force us out."

As they continued to pray, the evil forces finally cried out, "We knew about God the Father and the Son but we never met with God the Holy Spirit. Since he has come it's getting too hot for us. We've got to leave." Stegen reports that after the 300 demons left screaming through the sky, what had been the woman's ugly face dramatically changed. There was a heavenly smile as if she had been in the presence of Jesus for many years.

With this demonstration of God's power, Stegen's ministry took a radical turn. The strongholds of evil had been broken and the foundations of hell shaken. People started streaming to this little place of ministry, later called "Kwa-Siza Bantu," or "The Place of the Help People." Stegen reports that there would be 200 people standing on the garden lawn any time of the day, any day of the week.

"What do you want?" he would ask.

"We are sinners," they would reply. "We want peace with God. Can Jesus save us and forgive our sins?"

Lives were now being miraculously transformed. Husbands could no longer recognize their wives. "You used to be so stubborn I had to beat you with a rod," they would say. "Now you treat me like a king. What happened?"

As people spontaneously continued to pour in, sometimes thousands would be saved in one week. God's power was so great that the sick would occasionally be healed even before they were prayed for. In time, Stegen's group of co-workers increased to 70. They built an auditorium that would seat 3,000, but would often find it too small for the crowds that came day by day.

Ted Olsen recently visited the site of the revival and sent back a report. "They now have a hall," he wrote, "that seats about 15,000 and is full every weekend. Many people have come from other countries and taken the revival back with them. Flames have been lit around the world from the Zululand revival. The center where Stegen still lives and works is regularly the scene of healings and deliverances."

Is the Church ready for this?

As I ponder the significance of this revival taking place in just one small corner of one country in Africa, I wonder how we would handle it if and when something like this were to spread to whole countries and whole regions of the world. Will we be ready? Will we be equipped to lead great numbers to Christ? To train and disciple them? To enfold them into caring, healthy congregations? Will the Church have a tested and effective strategy already in operation? Will it be prepared to establish the tens of thousands, the hundreds of thousands, of new congregations for the host of converts?

Or will we be like the Church in Modesto, California, that had to "call off" the revival taking place in 1995 when 35,000 people came to Christ in a period of just eight weeks? Leaders soon realized they were totally unprepared to care for such a massive influx of new converts. (More on this in Chapter 8.)

When strongholds are broken as they were among the Zulu, when God answers the prayers literally of millions of intercessors around the world, when vast harvest fields such as those in China and the former Soviet Union are suddenly made available to us, when the time has fully come for the world revival we may already be in, will we be found with oil in our lamps? (Mt. 25:8).

When the demons that have enslaved massive populations are cast out and the house is clean, will we be ready to occupy it? Or will the forces of evil be allowed to return and the final condition be worse than the first? (Mt. 12:43-45).

Coleman puts this into perspective when he writes, "One more thing needs to be stressed. Prayer (for revival) leads to action. We cannot expect God to pour out His blessing unless we are willing to become involved in some kind of redemptive service."[10]

Our service to the Lord takes us in many directions, sometimes to the exclusion of our most cherished priorities. Coleman addresses this as well.

"Whatever form our service might take," he writes, "at its heart will be world evangelism—bringing all nations by all means to know Christ. If we are not occupied by this concern, we are a contradiction to the spirit of our loving Lord who came 'to seek and to save that which was lost' (Luke 19:10). It is silly to talk about going all the way with

Christ (in revival) when we are neglecting the work to which He gave His life."

With these comments, Coleman introduces the whole point of this book: since it is likely we are in the beginning stages, at least, of a mighty world revival, a revival that *could* lead to the completion of the Great Commission, what, then, should we do? What is the overall strategy this revival will empower for the completion of this awesome task in our time?

A strategy for the end of the age

Whatever the strategy, it must embody certain characteristics that intrinsically allow for a massive harvest and retention of that harvest.

In a revival situation, when great numbers are coming to the Lord and perhaps even greater numbers are ready to come, what would such a strategy look like? As in revival itself, I believe it would take us all the way back to the vision and strategy of the New Testament Church. In a book written in 1909 that Tom Phillips, President and CEO of International Students, refers to as one that "transcends time," there is a statement about revival that I believe is pertinent.

"First of all," writes author James Burns in *The Laws of Revival*, "we see that all revivals fall back on simplicity. They cut through the accumulated doctrines and subtle complexities, until they arrive at some aspect of truth which has become forgotten or has been buried by tradition.

"In perspective, every revival goes back to apostolic times and to the spirit of the early Church."[11]

While Burns is writing primarily about returning to the simple *message* of the cross, I do not think it inappropriate to suggest that what he writes should be true of the *methods* of the early Church as well.

Actually, the DAWN—Discipling A Whole Nation—

strategy we suggest in this book for the end of the age I believe takes us back to the dynamic of the early Church, a subject we will explore further in the next chapter. In fact, the power, eager acceptance and rapid spread of the DAWN/ saturation-church-planting idea surely stems at least in part from its very simplicity and biblical base.

More and more national and international leaders around the world are recognizing that activating and mobilizing the whole Body of Christ—all evangelical ministries—around the core idea of multiplying churches to a point of saturation in whole people groups and whole nations is the essence of simplicity for working at completing the Great Commission.

It is also a profound idea, carried out only with great effort in prevailing prayer, planning, implementing and persistence year after year. Yet, as I believe you will see throughout this book, it is a simple idea that can be traced "back to apostolic times and to the spirit of the early Church."

It cuts through the accumulated methodological baggage of centuries and arrives at an aspect of truth long forgotten or buried by tradition, to paraphrase Burns.

Looking beyond the year 2000

In my last book, *DAWN 2000: 7 Million Churches to Go*, the end of the second millennium was a point of reference only as a device to encourage more rapid church growth and the enfolding of a greater number of converts. This was a stimulant something like an industry trying to reach certain financial goals by the end of the year or John F. Kennedy setting a goal to reach the moon by the end of the 1960's decade.

If setting goals for such relatively minor milestones can focus resources and encourage higher productivity in the secular world, why should not such a major landmark date as the end of two thousand years of the Christian era challenge believers to a greater effort in their most important task? The very date itself should remind us that it's been 2,000 years—20 centuries!—since the Lord commanded us to "make disciples of all nations" and encourage us to evaluate how far we've come and how far we have to go.

Eight years after the last book, however, the emphasis here is no longer just on *hastening* our efforts but on actual *completion* of the task, whether this takes us to 2009, 2010, 2020 or beyond, even *way* beyond.

"God is at work throughout the earth to bring everything to consummation in Jesus Christ," wrote David Bryant in *The Hope at Hand*.[12] "...there appears to be a shared expectation that world revival is coming to bring closure to world evangelization and the consummation of all things."[13]

He also quotes J. Christy Wilson as saying, "I believe we've entered the fourth great awakening—it has already started—and it may be the last one. Because in this awakening God can complete his plan for the nations."

If these voices are truly a reflection of what is happening and what the Lord is saying to many of his chosen servants worldwide, we had better listen carefully and adjust our plans, activities and strategies accordingly.

With the evidence that we are in the time of the end, that the return of the Lord relatively is very close, that the consummation of the age is upon us, does this make a difference in how we think about the Great Commission? Does it suggest a different mindset from the previous 2,000 years? Does it require a paradigm shift in our doing missions and evangelism?

Peter Deyneka believes that it does. Likewise did Luke Huber before what the world would consider his untimely death. It seems to me their visions and strategies are in tune with what the Lord reveals in his Word and what many are recognizing as the strategy for the end of the age.

---

[1] Daniel 9:24.

[2] Harold E. Barton, *It's Here: The Time of the End* (New York: Exposition Press, 1963), p.24.

[3] Tom Phillips, *Revival Signs* (Gresham, OR: Vision House, 1995), p.223.

[4] James H. Montgomery, *DAWN 2000: 7 Million Churches to Go* (Pasadena, CA: William Carey Library, 1989), p.36.

[5] Listed in the *Yearbook of American & Canadian Churches, 1991* and reported in Whitten's "Toward the Year 2000, A National Forum on Evangelism and Church Planting," Aug, 1992.

[6] Source: Church Information Service, Japan, 1994.

[7] Source: Korea Ministry of Information, 1994.

[8] Robert E. Coleman, *The Coming World Revival* (Wheaton IL: Crossway Books, 1995), p.XIV.

[9] Out of print.

[10] Coleman, p.48.

[11] James Burns, Tom Phillips, editor, *The Laws of Revival* (Wheaton, IL: Worldwide Publications, 1993, in cooperation with the Institute of Evangelism, Billy Graham Center, Wheaton, IL), p.45.

[12] David Bryant, *The Hope At Hand* (Grand Rapids, MI: Baker Books, 1995), p.115.

[13] Ibid., p.125.

Chapter Two

His Glory Made Visible

All that is mine is yours, and that which is yours is mine; my glory is made visible in them.

John 17:10, translation from Spanish

Peter Deyneka came rushing up to me in the plush corridor of what had been Jimmy Baker's New Heritage Grand Hotel in South Carolina where the Evangelical Fellowship of Mission Agencies (EFMA) was holding its annual Executive Retreat.

"We really have DAWN underway in Russia now," he said with some excitement.

Comments like this happen so frequently that I almost expect them. But in Russia? I was skeptical until the whole story unfolded.

Sometime in 1988, my wife Lyn and I had breakfast with Peter and his wife, Anita. There was a lot of nostalgia as we talked about long-ago classmate days at Wheaton College. In the meantime, Peter, a Russian-American who speaks the language fluently, had ministered to Russia through radio from such diverse places as South America, Asia and Alaska.

Peter and Anita seemed to identify strongly with the DAWN vision as we explained it to them and suggested it might be implemented in at least one little nation of Eastern Europe. Then came six years of silence.

"In the last 23 months we have trained over 850 church planters in Russia," he was now telling me. "At least 600 of them have actually started a church!"

So far, so good. But there are over 300 million people in the former Soviet Union. How do we win millions of them and gather them into many thousands of evangelical congregations?

"Under Communism," he said, interrupting my thoughts, "there were sometimes five but as many as 40 potential pastors in each church. They were hemmed in by the system. Now there are tens of thousands of these young men who are potential church planters. They just need to be found and trained."

To meet this opportunity, Peter had launched a project called "Russia 250." The dream was to see 250 churches planted. With the explosive results in the first months, however, they kept the name but changed the game.

Now the goal is to establish 250 *training centers*, each covering a radius of 50 miles and located in all the nations of the former Soviet Union. The goal for *each* center is 250 churches, or a total of 62,500 new congregations in the next 25 years!

As of this writing, five of these centers are in operation and more than 1,000 churches and house groups that are turning into full churches have been established. They have a long way to go to reach their goals, of course, and whether they will or not will depend in part on what happens politically. My point here is that both the nature and scope of what they are attempting under the hand of the Lord is right on target.

Half a world away

Luke Huber, by contrast, was called to minister half a world away under completely different circumstances. I would like to have met this zealous young man who didn't want to miss a single soul in the 80,000 or so tiny villages of the vast rain forests of the Amazon River basin.

Growing up as a missionary kid in Brazil, Luke fell in love with the land and its people. He returned in 1976 to begin a ministry along the 4,000 miles of the mighty Amazon and its tributaries. He saw five Bible schools established, he developed quarterly training camps for pastors, he established a missionary orientation school and constructed a boat shop for building and repairing his primary transportation system for the region.

Above all, he planted churches and dreamed of planting more and more. His first goal was to start 100. This quickly changed to 1,000. Ultimately, he envisioned a church in every one of the 80,000 villages and another 20,000 in city neighborhoods and other parts of the Portuguese-speaking world.

His vision spread to others. After pioneering Project Amazon (PAZ, Portuguese for "peace"), family members started joining him. These included his parents and four siblings.

Other missionaries came on board, but none of these expatriates do the church planting. It's the national missionaries and pastors who have planted the first 300 churches and are committed to the goal of 1,700 more by AD 2000 and the long-range goal of 100,000.

Just as we were getting acquainted with Luke Huber through correspondence, he was killed when his ultra light sea plane crashed into the Amazon river after the conclusion of one of his beloved workers training sessions. At age 44, certainly in the prime years of his ministry, he left behind his wife Christine and four young children.

Christine Huber reports that her husband frequently said he wanted God to use his death, just as much as his life, to forward the Kingdom of God.

"People are taking responsibilities like never before," she says. "The assurance of God's presence is real, as we are reminded that the vision is the Lord's, not ours. The challenges are great, but we serve a great God."

PAZ leaders say the vision of 100,000 churches more than ever is on the tongues of everyone. "The pastors, missionaries and workers all over the river basin want to forward the Kingdom of God above all else," they report. "Hundreds of nationals are trained and ready, so the work is not going to slow down. A sense of excitement and expectancy grows each day. God is turning a tragic time of mourning into a time of joy."

The vision of SCP

Such personal tragedy and joy are a microcosm of a larger tragedy and joy. After many tragic centuries of darkness, the light of the gospel is finally beginning to reach the little villages of 50 to 100 people along the tributaries of the Amazon. After 70 years of satanic oppression, the joy of the Savior is entering multitudes of neighborhoods and villages of Russia and the republics of the former Soviet Union.

In just these two projects, there is now an actual, workable plan to see that the presence of the risen Christ is felt in the midst of people in more than 162,500 communities!

This is the methodology we have been calling "saturation church planting" (SCP). It is the vision of seeing the incarnate Christ present in the midst of every small unit of population in an area, in a country and in the world.

Though we didn't have a name for it at the time, this is the concept that became, and continues to be, the heart of the first DAWN project in the Philippines. What I felt the Lord saying to me about the Philippines in the 1970's I now hear being echoed around the world.

Where it came from

This SCP concept sounds simple and obvious now, but

for me it came only after 20 years of agonizing over how to go about making *disciples* of all *nations*. The whole story of seeking an optimum strategy for world evangelization is told in the book *DAWN 2000: 7 Million Churches to Go.*[1] One success after another was followed by one huge disappointment after another.

The climax came when the Christ the Only Way Movement came to an encouraging conclusion in the Philippines. In a very responsive land, virtually the whole Church was mobilized around the vision of seeing 10,000 evangelistic Bible study groups established, a method of proven value in this essentially Roman Catholic nation.

Then why wasn't I thrilled when the goal was actually surpassed? It was because out of 35 million Filipinos, there were still almost 35 million that did not have a personal relationship with the Lord. The account in *DAWN 2000* tells the resolution of the dilemma:

> "Why, Lord," I began to pray over a period of weeks, "did you give us a command that you knew was impossible to obey? Did you deceive us? Did you mean something different than what your Word seems clearly to say?
>
> "If you truly wanted *nations* to be *discipled*, why didn't you stay here on the earth? You could have gone about every village as you did in Galilee. You could have appeared speaking the language, wearing the dress, intimately knowing the culture, eating the food and having relatives and contacts in every village and neighborhood of every 'nation' in every country in the world.
>
> "You could have gone demonstrating your power, showing your love and compassion and forcefully communicating your great message of the Kingdom. Why did you leave it to us, when you knew it was totally beyond our capabilities?"
>
> "Now that I have your attention," the Lord seemed

to say after weeks of praying this prayer, "I want you to know that is exactly how to go about completing the Great Commission.

"See to it that I, the Lord, truly become incarnate, as you have been suggesting, in every small group of people on the earth."

In a flash of insight from the Lord it all became very clear. Where does the Lord dwell?

"Christ in you, the hope of glory" (Col. 1:27).

"...the one who is in you is greater than the one who is in the world" (1John 4:4).

"Where two or three come together in my name, there am I with them" (Mt. 18:20).[2]

It became clear that Christ could be alive and well and present in all his power and glory and compassion while communicating his wonderful message of the Kingdom in a totally contextualized way in every small community of people on Earth if only there were some truly born-again believers exercising the gifts of the Spirit and functioning in each place as the Body of Christ.

Shortly after my family and I completed our missionary stint in the Philippines in the mid 1970's, I happened to be talking with Dr. David Liao, then a professor of missions at Biola University. I told him about the dream and commitment of the Church in the Philippines to grow from about 5,000 congregations to 50,000 by the year AD 2000.

"Oh, you mean saturation church planting," he said.

I had followed the saturation *evangelism* movements such as Evangelism in Depth in Latin America, but I had never before heard the term saturation *church planting*.

But yes, that described exactly the concept that was developing in the Philippines. I had felt the Lord saying to me in 1974 that to work most directly at completing the Great Commission would mean seeing the risen Christ become incarnate within easy access of every person of every class, kind and condition of man in the world.

This translated into planting a Christ-centered church in the midst of every small group of people in every nation including all the "reached" and "unreached" people groups in each nation. To be even more specific, this would call for a cell of believers to be established in every village and city neighborhood, or a church for every 500 to 1,000 people.

Thus, saturation church planting—SCP—became the essence of the strategy we suggest for completing the Great Commission, the strategy for the end of the age.

That is why in establishing Dawn Ministries in 1985 we wrote our purpose statement to say that our calling was "...to see saturation church planting become the generally accepted and fervently practiced strategy for completing the task of making disciples of all peoples in our generation."

Seeing SCP in the Bible

I am aware, of course, that the validity of a strategy for world evangelization depends on much more than my testimony and what seems to work. Though my gifting is not as a scholar or theologian, I am encouraged by the fact that over the past 20 years of the existence and spread of the DAWN strategy, I have yet to hear a theologian speak against it. Actually, the reverse has been true. I frequently come across comments of theologians and missiologists that tend to reinforce that which I felt I heard from the Lord or learned from godly mentors.

This is not to say that I did not find support for the SCP concept from my own Bible study. Take the ministry of the Apostle Paul, for example. While his methods varied and were highly contextualized, the fruit of his ministry was powerfully consistent: there were always strings of multiplying congregations permeating large populated areas left behind. It could then be said "that all the Jews and Greeks who lived in...Asia heard the word of the Lord" (Acts 19:10).

As Peter Wagner wrote in *Spreading the Fire* (his first of three volumes in "The Acts of the Holy Spirit" series), "The most concrete, lasting form of ministry in Acts is church planting. Preaching the gospel, healing the sick, casting out demons, suffering persecution, holding church councils and multiple other activities of the apostles and other Christians that unfold before us have, as their goal, multiplying Christian churches throughout the known world."[3]

In the third volume of this series, Wagner also wrote, "Part of Paul's influence in the new churches was, undoubtedly, to stir them to evangelize the lost in their cities and to plant new house churches in every neighborhood. *No missiological principle is more important than saturation church planting...*" (italics mine).[4]

Later, I began to connect this multiplication of churches with an Old Testament vision and prophecy that was repeated in at least four books of the Bible.

Numbers 14:21, for example, records that "...all the earth shall be filled with the glory of the Lord" (RSV) Similar prophecies are recorded in Isaiah 11:9 and Habakkuk 2:14.

A few months ago, Luis Bush, International Director of the massive AD2000 and Beyond Movement, pointed out to me the last two verses of Psalm 72. Verse 20 says "This concludes the prayers of David son of Jesse." And what were the last words of the last prayer of David? "...may the whole earth be filled with his glory. Amen and Amen" (vs. 19).

Where does the glory of the Lord reside? Certainly "The heavens declare the glory of God; the skies proclaim the work of his hands" (Ps. 19:1). But many verses also tell us that Christ—and therefore his glory—resides in us.

Even while writing this chapter I saw this again as I was meditating and praying through the priestly prayer of our

Lord recorded in John 17. As I was reading in my Spanish Bible, *"...mi gloria se hace visible en ellos,"* suddenly jumped from the page (vs. 10).

"My glory is made visible in them."

There it was again! More than planting churches, more than saving souls, we yearn for the day when it can truly be said that the earth *is* full of the glory of the Lord. And where is his glory? "My glory is made visible in *them*." In his people.

Peter Wagner also picks up on this in *Spreading the Fire* mentioned above when he writes that "...multitudes of churches in many parts of the world, although imperfectly, do accurately reflect the glory of God through Jesus Christ...."[5]

SCP, then, is simply the task of seeing that there is the presence of Christ in every place in the form of a gathered body of believers.

Even so, we work at saturation church planting not only because it is a good strategy for completing the Great Commission. We do it because we want to cooperate with the oft-repeated Old Testament prophecy that "...the earth will be filled with the knowledge of the glory of the Lord" (Hab. 2:14 etc.).

We do it to answer the last recorded prayer of David: "...may the whole earth be filled with his glory" (Ps. 72:19).

We do it so that the glory of the Lord may be made visible in every small community of mankind in the world.

Every place you set your foot

Another Old Testament preview of the Great Commission, I have come to believe, is the book of Joshua. While the circumstances are quite different, the principles of how to *conquer* a nation and how to *disciple* a nation do not seem to be that far apart. For the Israelites, the strategy was to go city by city and nation by nation and actually *take possession* of the land.

"Go through the camp," Joshua was told, "and tell the people, 'Get your supplies ready. Three days from now you will cross the Jordan here to go in and *take possession* of the land the Lord your God is giving you for your own'" (1:11).

Their job was not just to defeat an army or just to take a city here and there. They were to occupy every square meter of the land. The Lord told Joshua, "I will give you every place where you set your foot, as I promised Moses" (1:3).

He was even told exactly what territory he would occupy. This would include all the Hittite country from the Mediterranean Sea all the way to the Euphrates River. To emphasize the point, Joshua 12 records precisely all 31 of the nations that had already been conquered and occupied. Then the next chapter with equal precision records all the places that remained where Joshua and the Israelites had yet to set their feet. Can we compare these with the so-called "reached" and "unreached" peoples and nations of the world, nations in both categories that still need to be *fully* occupied?

To compare this with modern warfare, their mission was not just to send in bombers to flatten all the enemy fortifications and level their cities. They needed foot soldiers to invade the territory, drive the enemy completely out and occupy the countryside and every village, town and city.

Likewise, the vision of Saturation Church Planting is to *occupy* all the nations and peoples of the world by establishing cells of committed believers in every small community of mankind.

When we are working at filling the earth with communities of believers, when we are planting churches everywhere, we are cooperating with both the Old and New Testament concepts of how to make disciples of all nations.

SCP and winning the lost

Every once in a while we come across a church growth plan where the goal is set in terms of a certain number of new converts to be made. On the surface, it makes sense. Jesus died for lost sinners, so why not aim at winning as many as possible, or winning a certain number by a certain date?

Ask the Christian and Missionary Alliance Convention in the Philippines. In the first 75 years of this century they planted 477 churches. This was good, but certainly not extraordinary growth. After the Church Growth Workshop in 1974 when the DAWN vision was first presented, they set a healthy goal of planting 400 more churches in just four years.

With tremendous zeal and energy, they mobilized their whole denomination as well as their parent C&MA mission around this vision. You can imagine the great rejoicing when they actually exceeded their goal by starting 416 new churches and more than doubling their membership from 26,830 to 58,543 in this four-year period. This increase represented a very strong Average Annual Growth Rate (AAGR) of 13 percent for church planting and quite a remarkable 21.5 percent AAGR for new members.

With the enthusiasm generated by this great leap forward, they developed a new program called "Target 100,000 '83."

This time, there was great consternation when they fell 20,000 members short of their goal. Analyzing what happened, they realized the mistake they made was in aiming at the number of converts they would win—bringing their total membership to 100,000—instead of the evangelistic activity—church planting—that would bring in the converts. In their next project, they reinstated church planting as their primary target and evangelistic activity.

Naturally, our desire is to bring as many to know Christ as personal savior as possible. God is not wanting anyone to perish (IIPet.3:9). But in developing an actual strategy, we have found it better to set our sights on the activity that will bring the greatest number to the Lord rather than on the number to be won.

Research following the first DAWN Congress in England led to the same conclusion.

"That C. Peter Wagner was right when he asserted in 1992 that 'church planting is the most effective evangelistic method under heaven in all contexts and at all times' has again been proven true." So states "Planting for a Harvest," the DAWN Resource Manual prepared for Challenge 2000 and the Second England DAWN Congress in March, 1995.[6]

The manual refers to research done in the 1970's by Anglican David Wasdell. His data established a diminishing effectiveness in Anglican Churches as their parish size grew. His conclusion that parishes should become multi-centered with several congregations taking responsibility for sections of the total community sadly was not acted upon, states the manual.

In the last three years, however, three other research projects in England have all demonstrated that Wasdell was right.

In a survey of 350 churches conducted by Challenge 2000, the DAWN England project, for example, the 64 churches planted since 1989 had grown on average by over 75 percent per year! By contrast, even the strong evangelical/charismatic churches established prior to that date were increasing by just 6 percent a year.

"In other words," states the manual, "the new church plants in our survey were **growing 12 times as fast as established churches!**"

The Challenge 2000 survey also knocked in the head the fear that starting new congregations tends to retard the growth of the parent congregation.

"The survey showed that the 55 churches which had given birth to new churches had grown on average 31.5 percent between 1990 and 1994," the manual reported. "The non-planting churches grew on average 19.6 percent in the same period."

A table that appeared in the manual also supports Wagner's contention that planting churches is the best method for gaining new converts in any context.

It indicates that 68 percent of the growth in these new congregations was from conversions and renewals and only 25 percent was from transfers. This pattern was similar in all seven environments ranging from cities to remote rural areas and from resorts to new towns.

If our concern—as it should be—is to win the greatest number possible to Christ, the evidence indicates we should major in planting churches from among the unconverted.

SCP and the unreached

What happens when there are few, if any believers in a people group, when there is persecution of any known Christians, when any churches that do exist are forced to meet in secret? Is it rational even to think of *multiplying* congregations?

Absolutely! My viewpoint is that if we do not go into a situation with the vision of SCP for a people group, we will perhaps never find the strategy that will result in a host of churches being planted. If our expectation is that it will take years or even decades to start multiplying churches, then that is how long it will take.

For example, while visiting in Egypt a few months ago, Steve Steele, CEO for Dawn Ministries, was told about a short-term team of Egyptian believers that was sent to another North African nation. Their assignment was to plant a church from among Muslim converts.

"That will take many years," they were told on arrival by local believers.

"But we only have two months," they responded. "We must plant a church before we go back."

And they did! Had their expectation been otherwise,

they would never have found the key to church planting in that situation.

It seems to me that unless missionaries and strategists to the Muslim world are dreaming of planting one million churches—whatever they might look like—for the one billion Muslims, they would be unnecessarily prolonging the discipling of those nations. I'm not saying the task would be easy. I'm not saying there would not be martyrs in the process. I *am* saying unless there is a vision and a goal of planting one million churches from Muslim converts, the way will never be found to do it.

In another predominantly Islamic setting that we dare not even mention by name, a strategy is being implemented where thousands of "churches" are being planted. They do not look like churches, they are not even called "churches." But they are! And the leaders involved are committed to the SCP vision. They are working out a plan to fill this whole nation with cells of believers in the Lord Jesus Christ.

Rev. B.A.G. Prasad, who, until the Lord took him home in 1994, was Director of Every Home for Christ in India, had a similar vision and plan for reaching Hindus in India. Years of dynamic ministry saw evangelical literature delivered twice to virtually every household in the country. As a result, over five million Indians filled out a card indicating their decision to accept Jesus Christ. It disturbed Prasad, however, that India was still only 2.6 percent Christian, the same as when the ministry started 28 years before.

This called for a change in strategy. Instead of EHC national missionaries merely leaving literature in as many homes and as many villages as was possible in a day, they now focus on planting churches. When they go to a home, they try to determine if any family member is interested in the gospel. If there is such a person, they stay as long as necessary to lead him or her to Christ. Then it is around this new convert that ultimately a "Christ group" or small house church is developed.

In this program, now called "Final Thrust 5000," they have set a goal for 300,000 house churches by AD 2000!

In a stirring message delivered at the EHC World Congress Banquet some months before his death, Prasad explained that "We call it 'Final' because we believe the Lord is coming soon. We call it '5,000' because we determined that is the number of national missionaries we need for 300,000 new churches."

He explained that India is divided into 400 districts and that it would take 10 missionaries to cover each district. That would call for 4,000 missionaries and perhaps another 1,000 for training and administration. Hence the total of 5,000.

God has really blessed this new approach which was launched in July of 1992. Eighteen months later they already had 1,500 missionaries in place which were performing hundreds of baptisms in about 500 new churches a month. Most of these were house-type churches, but some were thriving with 200 to 300 members. The ministry was empowered with such miracles as three who were raised from the dead, one after five hours.

"We are praying that before Christ comes India will be a Christian nation," Prasad told the conferees. With his passing, the movement slowed somewhat. In 1995, however, another 1,750 house churches were established and the project is again on the upswing.

There is another powerful story coming out of the world of Hindus that illustrates this point. The missionary doctor involved is not only reaching Hindus, but he is, incredibly, reaching them *with* Hindus! We'll get his story in Chapter Seven.

SCP as 'Outside-in' thinking

Another strong proponent and excellent teacher of the SCP vision of working towards the goal of filling all nations with dynamic, evangelical congregations is Dwight Smith, former president of United World Mission and now founder and president of SCP International. He refers to SCP as "outside-in" thinking.

Usually, a local or denominational body thinks of growth in just the opposite fashion, he teaches. It thinks in terms of how big it is and what it must do to get a little bigger. Outside-in thinking turns the process around. It draws a circle around a neighborhood, a city, a province, a people group or a whole nation and works back from there. It asks the question, "What would it take to win this whole harvest field for the Lord?"

As a friend of ours who owns a major business says in layman's terms, "We need to look at the total industry. The whole body of Christ of the whole nation needs to look at the total problem. That is strategy. It is only valid if you have a forum for all the players."

Perhaps I can best illustrate this concept by relating the testimony of Freddie Gwanzura, a local pastor in Zimbabwe.

In 1976 Gwanzura left his building contractor's business and became a full-time worker with the Apostolic Faith Mission. Soon he was pastoring a congregation of 60 on the outskirts of a town. The church building seated a few hundred, but nothing he tried would increase his attendance.

About this time, Reinhardt Bonkke, the German evangelist, held a crusade in the area. He pitched his tent that held 10,000 people just one kilometer from the church. This gave Freddie immediate hope. He was certain his church would grow dramatically as a result of the crusade! The tent was full every night. People came and repented in the thousands.

After the crusade, his church did the followup and tried their best to keep the fish in the net, but there were few lasting results. A year later he reports there was one woman attending he thought was won at the crusade. But they were still a church of 60 members.

"The one benefit of the crusade," Freddie Gwanzura told us, "was that we had learned the hard way that we could not project our responsibility to evangelize and see the church grow on a visiting evangelist. So we began to do our own evangelism and followup, using every kind of method the Lord gave us. Even funeral services became an outreach opportunity."

Gradually, the pews of his church began to fill. They had to move into the church yard as their attendance grew from 60 to about 400. By 1982, they began to realize they would have to plant new churches. The first one was in a nearby town. They spun off some of their people from the main fellowship. They thought this would give them breathing room, but within one week they were full again! So, here and there, they planted still more new churches.

But Freddie says that "By the time the DAWN consultation came to our area, however, I knew something was still missing. My vision was not complete. DAWN changed all this. I had my eyes opened to the importance of research and good information. I had no idea how big my harvest field was, how many villages or towns were in it. I had not looked to see where there were churches or where there were no churches. DAWN showed me how to look at my province, my section of the harvest field. The Lord caused me to see that the existing churches were a drop in the bucket in terms of what we needed. I realized that our job would not be done until there was a church there for everybody."

Today, Freddie has over 200 churches under his supervision. DAWN thinking is at the heart of his work. The message that he wants his life to communicate to the men under his leadership is: "We must plant churches! This is the vision that possesses me. Planting new congregations in all the villages and growth points in our province is the main thing God wants us to do."

When Gwanzura stopped thinking just about how to

increase his membership and began looking at the harvest field of his whole province, he had switched from inside-out thinking to outside-in. He had caught the vision of saturation church planting.

Universal application

There are outstanding examples of this SCP/outside-in thinking all over the world and at every level.

A local church can do SCP. For instance, the Woodmen Valley Chapel where we live in Colorado Springs has begun a project to establish 500 TLC groups—Tiny Little Churches. These would blanket the city and provide what in effect would be one "house church" for every 600 local residents. Yong-gi Cho's church in Korea has saturated Seoul with 70,000 similar groups!

An excellent SCP project on a national level is the One, One, One project developed by Chris Marantika in Indonesia. He has drawn a circle "outside" the whole nation. His concept is ultimately to establish 415 seminaries providing instruction at various academic levels. All students are required to plant a church before graduation and are trained to go on to multiply new churches after that. The vision is to establish *one* church in each *one* village in *one* generation.[7]

Anybody can develop an SCP project, but it will take everybody doing it to complete the Great Commission in our time. As Leighton Ford has observed, "If our goal is the penetration of the whole world, then...we must aim at nothing less than the mobilization of the whole church."[8]

If every Western and non-Western mission society, every one of 22,000 denominations in the nations of the world, every para-church ministry and every local church and every intercessory network caught this vision, there is no question but that "filling the earth with the knowledge of the glory of the Lord" by the presence of a local congregation for every cluster of people would be easily within our reach by AD 2010. Or way before!

This is the vision that must drive our prayers and our activities if we are to see the close of the age in our time.

Easier said than done, of course! How do we go about infusing the *whole* Church of the *whole* world with such a vision and mobilizing it for such a task? That's where the DAWN strategy comes in. It was developed for this very purpose. To get a clearer idea of how it works, we'll now take a look at a project that in a few short years has completely turned around the decades-long decline of the Church in England.

---

[1] James H. Montgomery, *DAWN 2000: 7 Million Churches to Go* (Pasadena, CA: William Carey Library, 1989).

[2] Ibid., pp. 29, 30.

[3] C. Peter Wagner, *Spreading the Fire* (Ventura, CA: Regal Books, 1994), p.60.

[4] C. Peter Wagner, *Blazing the Way* (Ventura, CA: Regal Books, 1995), p.48.

[5] C. Peter Wagner, *Spreading the Fire*, p.60.

[6] Available from Dawn Ministries.

[7] This project is described in full in *DAWN 2000: 7 Million Churches to Go*.

[8] Robert E. Coleman, *The Coming World Revival* (Wheaton, IL: Crossway Books, 1989), p.86.

Chapter Three

England: Modeling the Strategy

'I believe we are in the most exciting moment the Christian church has ever experienced.'

Roger Forster
Founder of March for Jesus

Like so many of the 100 or so DAWN projects currently underway, DAWN England sprang to life when one man almost instantaneously caught the vision. In this case, it was Lynn Green, Director for Europe, Africa and the Middle East for Youth With A Mission.

In another surprising twist, Green was an American living in London. But in his 25 years of ministry there he had so served the leaders and integrated himself into the life of the Church that he was accepted as one of their own. He had also become quite visible through his development of March For Jesus. This ministry really caught on in England and then spread around the world with the result that about 11 million participated in various nations in 1994.

"One of the major roots of the DAWN strategy in England was actually March For Jesus," Green said to me in a recorded interview. "I had this friendship with Gerald Coates (Director of Pioneer, a major church-planting movement), Roger Forster (evangelist and founder of Icthus Fellowship), and Graham Kendrick (musician and prolific song writer). As far as I know, we were each independently beginning to engage in praise walks or mobile prayer meetings. We were going out on the streets as part of the preparation of a neighborhood or a town for evangelism.

"I think Graham was the catalyst who suggested we ought to unite our efforts in one larger prayer walk," Green told me. "The idea clicked. When we discovered Roger had someone in his congregation that had access to Smithfield's Meat Market, we mobilized our respective forces for a grand gathering in that area. Our hope was that 5,000 might show up. Instead, 15,000 came. That was the beginning of March for Jesus."

These leaders and strategic thinkers had been friends for years, but this first March for Jesus in 1987 drew them even closer together. The huge turnout was beyond their expectation. They recognized something special was happening that they wanted to pursue.

"When we got together afterwards," Green said, "we found that we shared in common a deep desire for saturation evangelism. But we didn't have a strategic context for it. We spent a lot of time talking, thinking and praying together. 'Lord, what is this all about?' we were asking."

Out of these prayer and brainstorming sessions emerged what this informal group thought of as a vision statement: "By AD 2000, every person in England would have repeatedly heard the gospel in a form they would listen to and understand."

"That summarized what we thought God wanted to happen," says Green. "But how to do it? We didn't know."

This is it!

The answer came in an instant of recognition when Green and a number of other Church leaders from England attended the first Global Consultation on World Evangelization held in Singapore in February of 1989. Out of this would emerge the AD 2000 and Beyond Movement headed by Luis Bush.

I didn't remember that I had a speaking role in this consultation until Green reminded me.

"When I heard you share the DAWN strategy," he said, "it just clicked. I thought, 'That's it! That's the bigger, strategic picture. That's the obvious biblical approach. That is the only way to see the Great Commission accomplished and—more importantly—remain accomplished.'"

Green immediately saw that this was the strategy that could get everyone to pull together in what had been declared as the decade of evangelism in England. He also intuitively knew that he would have to get some kind of consensus among the shapers of opinion in the country. Of all the leaders he spoke with while still in Singapore, however, only Roger Forster responded with a resounding affirmation.

"I left the Consultation somewhat discouraged," Green told me, "but on the way home I read your book *DAWN 2000: 7 Million Churches to Go*. This convinced me all the more that this was the strategy we needed to again reach our nation for Christ."

Back in England, things got worse before they got better. Other members of their informal group quickly embraced the DAWN idea, though there was some concern that talk of church planting would tarnish the interdenominational, non-threatening image of March for Jesus. Once the whole concept was fully understood, however, the issue disappeared.

There was still need for a broader consensus, however. To gain this, a group of 90 key leaders were called for a one-day consultation after the March for Jesus rally in 1989. That's where the blow fell.

The meeting started out well enough when these leaders were given a chance to evaluate and give their input on the direction for March for Jesus. Then Green was given a chance to present the DAWN strategy with the hope that consensus would now emerge for this national project.

"As I did so, I just felt resistance," Green told me. "It was so difficult, one of the hardest meetings I was ever in. I could see that somehow I was not getting all the ingredients together well enough for them to appreciate the concept.

"Then one of the guys who is a specialist in church planting said, 'You're advocating church planting. Now what model of church planting are we talking about? There are 12.' I lost it."

Not a lost cause

Though Green was sure the cause was lost, the reverse was happening. He later learned that he actually had a lot of support, that many didn't like what was happening when the "experts" tore apart a vision before there was really a chance to explain it.

With the encouragement of his core group of friends, Green sent out another letter of invitation to the same group of leaders for a three-day consultation. This time, the invitation boldly spelled out the DAWN concept as the topic for discussion rather than tagging it on to another topic.

To their delight, 60 of these leaders came, listened to Dawn Ministries missionary Johan Combrinck (now president of AFnet) as well as Green, Forster and others. This time, the response was overwhelmingly positive!

Given the opportunity, this group asked questions, made suggestions and came up with adaptations. "We went away and looked at the recommendations," Green explained, "saw how often they were repeated and chose from them. What we were trying to do was find the balance between taking the lead and at the same time listening and giving people the opportunity to help shape the strategy. In the process, these key leaders gained a lot of ownership for the vision."

They also recommended people for a steering committee that would be responsible for the first DAWN Congress to be held in Birmingham in April, 1992. This date was set far enough away so that there was time to get denominational leaders on board, to promote the Congress, to form all the necessary committees and carry out the myriad details connected with such a major national gathering. Chris Forster, son of Roger, accepted the role as full-time coordinator and Green saw to it that YWAM staff members made this a priority. Leadership was now mobilized to launch a Discipling A Whole Nation project for England with a national Congress "that would be a resounding success," according to Green.

There were also, of course, the research to be done and the prophetic message to be developed. These are the heart and soul of the DAWN process and will be referred to again.

The Steering Committee, by the way, chose the name "Challenge 2000" for their project. This is significant to mention as there is sometimes confusion between Dawn Ministries the organization and DAWN the strategy. Dawn Ministries, as I write elsewhere, does not sponsor any national project. We do give the DAWN strategy away to be used by any sponsoring body. The steering committee in England handled this nicely when they explained in their congress manual that 'Challenge 2000' is an initiative promoting the DAWN strategy."

The 20/20 vision

When initial research was completed, the newly appointed Steering Committee met for several days of prayer and fasting to determine what the Lord was saying to them about a national goal.

"Ultimately, we concluded the Lord would have us trust him for 20,000 new congregations by the end of the decade," Green told me. "As we thought about that, we realized many more people would come to know the Lord and come into our churches. With this many new congregations, we determined that those attending church would make up about 20 percent of the population.

"For us, this was a big step of faith in a country where the Church had been in decline for many decades.

"To test whether we were hearing from the Lord, we shared this goal with no one. Then, at the Congress itself, we sent the various denominational groups off by themselves to seek God, to strategize and to make some faith commitments. How many churches did they feel their denomination should plant in the next eight years?

"After the denominational streams met together and reported back, we added all their individual goals and discovered they totaled just over 20,000! We realized that God had put his stamp of approval on the strategy.

"So we developed the goal statement: There would be 20,000 new churches and 20 percent of the population attending church by the end of the 20th century: 20/20 vision."

I was naturally thrilled when the first DAWN England Congress, sponsored by what had become a structure called "Challenge 2000," settled on the twin goals of adding 20,000 new congregations and seeing 20 percent of the population in church on a Sunday morning.

Becoming a movement

Such great news, however, had to be tempered with reality. Setting a challenging goal is not the same as reaching it. Furthermore, a DAWN project is not just one event or even a series of events. Rather, it is a long-range process. It is a repeating cycle of research, national congresses, national goals set, denominational plans made and implemented, progress evaluated toward the goals set at every level and then starting over again. It is a healthy rhythm to be continued until the Lord comes again. It is an attempt to see effective evangelism and saturation church planting become part of the psyche, part of the regular, budgeted, staffed activities of every denomination and local congregation.

So while Lynn Green and the rest of the Steering Committee could rejoice in the "success" of the first DAWN Congress, the real work was yet to begin. From the Congress, they sent out denomination heads and leaders of various other church-planting streams to put their goals into action.

Nor could the committee relax from its labors. There was now the task of spreading the vision further, of tracking what was being accomplished, of reporting this in a periodical that had to be developed, of determining the strengths and weaknesses of the movement and of preparing for the next congress based on what they were learning. All this and much, much more would require fund raising, office setup, staffing and so on.

In many respects, holding a second DAWN Congress is more significant than the first. For one thing, it shows there was enough interest in the concept even to go through all the pains of a national conference all over again. But in a second congress, you find out if the concept has taken hold. You look for signs of growing momentum. You begin to see if there is a self-perpetuating movement underway or if you've just had another set of good activities.

I was very encouraged, for example, when the Church in the Philippines held twin congresses in Cebu and Baguio cities in 1980, five years after I had left the country as a resident missionary. It was even more fulfilling to attend their *fifth* congress in February of 1994 and to learn they were now planning a congress every two years until the end of the century!

Each congress adds depth to the movement. New theological and biblical insights are gained and shared. Effective church-planting projects are highlighted. Up-to-date research creates new enthusiasm as increased growth rates are unveiled, or new challenge is given when data indicates areas of concern. The Church sees how far it has come in reaching national and denominational goals and how far it still has to go. Each congress includes delegates who have never attended before so more and more leaders are involved and the next generation is being brought on board.

The second and subsequent congresses provide opportunity to make mid-course corrections for the movement. After the first flush of excitement in a unified strategy to reach its whole nation, the Church also begins to take a more serious look at the unreached peoples in its nation, in helping with DAWN projects in neighboring nations and even in the pioneer missionary task of hidden peoples in far-off lands.

Of great significance also is the growing unity of the body of Christ—by which the world shall know to whom we belong—is fostered. I saw this profoundly in the fifth congress in the Philippines. Gone were the early days of suspicion, posturing, shouting, criticizing and braggadocio. All this was visibly replaced with a joy, almost an hilarity, as the 200 or so leaders laughed and rejoiced and applauded together at what the Lord was doing.

Jun Vencer captured this in his observation that "Leaders in the Philippines are no longer saying that *we* have 500 churches but *we* have 35,000." At last and for once the Body of Christ in a nation was perceiving itself as a body and not as individual, isolated, competing entities.

'DAWN is dawning, the sun is rising!'

If there were any doubts that DAWN had taken root in English soil, they were soon dispelled by the Second DAWN Congress held in Nottingham, March 7-9, 1995. All of the above was happening and much more.

Even The Most Reverend Dr. George Carey—Archbishop of Canterbury and who is head of the world-wide Anglican Communion—gave his wholehearted endorsement to the movement. Anglican Bishop Pat Harris told congress delegates that the Archbishop is very committed to the whole concept of church planting and of the need for discipling the whole nation.

To many observers, such a statement coming from the head of the Church of England is truly astounding. It would be expected that a state-supported Church based on the parish system would conclude that no more churches are needed, that the church-planting job was done years ago.

"Church planting is proving to be one of the most exciting developments in this decade of evangelism," Carey said in a statement read at the Congress. "In many parts of this country we are seeing these adventures of faith resulting in genuine numerical growth. May this Congress help us all to listen and to learn from each other as we seek to proclaim Christ to this generation."

Reports at the congress indicate that there had indeed been genuine "adventures of faith."

"There has been a huge change in the official position of many denominations towards the issue of church planting," reported Chris Forster, Director of the Challenge 2000 (DAWN) project.

"At the time of the first Congress," he continued, "the Assemblies of God and the Salvation Army were on their way to official church-planting policy and goals. Since that time, *every other major Protestant denomination in England has adopted a church-planting policy and in some cases set a specific target.*"

The Methodist Church, for one, set a goal to plant at least one church in every one of their approximately 650 circuits!

Furthermore, as the Archbishop suggests, these adventures in faith have resulted in "genuine numerical growth."

The Assemblies of God, for example, are now ahead of schedule in reaching their goal of 1,000 new churches by AD 2000. In 1994 they were planting six new churches every week! The Baptist Union has planted 70 new churches and the Methodists about 40.

The Salvation Army opened 57 new works in England and the rest of Great Britain in just two years. One local church, Kensington Temple, has planted about 90 daughter congregations since 1990, is now planting two or three a month and has a goal of 2,000 new churches by the year 2000!

The most incredible turn around, however, had to be the Church of England itself. This staid and static state Church that had been declining by about eight percent a year for several decades was now reportedly starting one new congregation a week!

"Our careful DAWN research now indicates that in the first five years of this decade," Forster reported, "over 1,500 churches were started, the majority being in 1992 and 1993 (since the first DAWN Congress)."

Furthermore, as we reported in the last chapter, these new church plants were growing 12 times as fast as established churches, mother churches were growing 50 percent faster than childless ones, and 68 percent of the growth in these new congregations was from conversions and renewals!

The actual numbers of churches being planted are not to be compared with many third-world DAWN projects where explosive new church planting is measured by the thousands. But for evangelical leaders of England, this news shared with the 970 delegates representing virtually every major denomination in the nation at the second Congress was nothing short of electrifying. Though it was acknowledged they were still not growing fast enough to reach the 1992 goals of 20,000 new churches and 20 percent of the population in church, they recognized that something of historic proportions was taking place.

Roger Forster, head of the mushrooming Ichthus Fellowship, captured this mood in the opening remarks of his address.

"The dawn is dawning!" he exclaimed. "The sun is rising. The fire of God is burning! The wind of God is blowing! *Something* is happening anyway! The tide is coming in at last. I believe we are in the most exciting moment the Christian church has ever experienced.

"We're moving to that great moment when we'll hear a real trumpet blast. This good news will be preached in all the world and the end will come. I don't think that we've ever been nearer than we are now. I believe that what is happening in the world is affecting us here in the UK, as we will see as this conference moves along."

That the DAWN strategy was not merely an ivory tower idea dreamed up by gung ho American pragmatists but rather was deeply rooted both in Scripture and the whole history of the Church in England became clearer and clearer as the Congress progressed.

Centrality of the local church

Chris Forster, son of Roger Forster quoted above and representative of those very bright, high energy, deeply committed "John Knoxers" emerging in nation after nation around the world, shared his own biblical insights on the DAWN strategy:

> The importance of planting churches in relation to the growth that we are seeing worldwide is incredibly tied in," he said in a plenary session. "The DAWN strategy grew out of the experience of the Church in the Philippines, but since that time it has moved to over 85 nations. And this is the strategy which you have heard Peter Wagner say "is the best delivery system that we have for taking the theoretical church growth principles and helping them to be applied in the pews and in

the grass roots and reaching out in evangelism in a particular nation."

Why is DAWN so successful? I think first of all it is founded on the importance of the local church in mission. This is a biblical principle. When Jesus came he did most of the ministry. He evangelized thousands, he fed 5,000, he healed the sick. Then he gave the commission and he left 120 people meeting in a room to complete it. Then the Holy Spirit fell on them and the Church was born.

The Church is the implement. The Church is the body which God has ordained to fulfill its great commission.

The early Church so much believed in the importance of the local church that even as it grew to 3,000, 10,000 and upwards in Jerusalem it continued to meet from house to house. They saturated the city of Jerusalem with what we might call cell groups or neighborhood churches. When the persecution came, they scattered throughout Judea and Samaria, establishing new little bodies of believers in every village.

Acts 18 records that when Paul got to Corinth, he evangelized among one particular people group, the Jews. He had little success there so in effect he said, "I'm not only going to the Jews, I'm going to the Gentiles. To do that, I'm going to move next door to the house of Titius Justice because that is a place the Gentile community can identify with. They won't identify with the synagogue, but they will with the house of Titius Justice."

He understood the importance of that local, contextualized working out of the body of Jesus. That is why I believe DAWN is successful. It puts responsibility for mission back into the local church. That is what we want to see and what is beginning to happen in our own nation.

DAWN began in AD 685!

Congress speakers found DAWN not only imbedded in the authority of the Scriptures but also found it deeply rooted in the past and current history of the Church in England.

Bishop Pat Harris, who represented Archbishop Carey at the Congress, centered his remarks around the published two-fold purpose of DAWN England:

1. To provide Christ-centered, evangelizing cells, congregations or churches for every village and neighborhood of every class, kind and condition of person in the country.

2. To develop a systematic plan to make sure that every person in our nation hears the gospel in a relevant form by the strategic planting of new churches and mobilizing of local evangelism.

"I want to develop those two aims because I believe they reflect and repeat the way the gospel broke new ground in England well over a thousand years ago," he began. "It is good for us to remember our heritage and it's good to remind ourselves that what we are doing today is based on good principles that have already been proven in our land."

"If we want an early DAWN model of planting local, Christ-centered, evangelizing cells," he said, "we have it in St. Cuthbert and the Celtic missionaries who came down from northern England in the 7th century. When he arrived in the South in AD 685, Cuthbert did not confine his teaching and influence to one geographical area but walked far and near, challenging ordinary folk to exchange their superstition, profanity and wickedness for a love of the heavenly joys."

The historian Jean-Albert Bédé was quoted as writing that "Cuthbert had such a love for proclaiming his message that he used to visit and preach in the villages that lay far distant among high and inaccessible mountains which others feared to visit."

In more recent centuries, Harris pointed out that "this historic precedent for the DAWN strategy in Britain can also be seen in the Anglican Church. Those of us who happen to be in the Church of England have treasured what is known as the 'parish principle.' Sadly, this has frequently been seen primarily as a question of territory and geographical boundaries. But the parish principle is basically a strategy for mission. It emphasizes the responsibility for Christian witness to all who live in *any* neighborhood and *every* neighborhood. That is why there is a commitment not just to parish churches in the cities and towns but also in the village and rural areas as well."

Flocking to their usual haunts

Bishop Harris also developed the second DAWN England purpose of strategically multiplying new churches that would present the gospel in a *relevant* form for every Englishman. This builds on the basic DAWN concept of providing a local congregation for every city neighborhood and rural village *for every class, kind and condition of man*. There was historical precedent for this in England as well.

"In the south of England," he said, "the Roman missionaries pursued an action plan Gregory gave Augustine of Canterbury in AD 601. It was an approach different from Cuthbert's. It involved adapting the way the good news was communicated to take seriously the culture of the people. For example, heathen temples were not to be destroyed. They were to be purified from the worship of demons and dedicated to the service of the true God. In this way, Gregory hoped, the people would come flocking to their usual haunts but to know and adore the true God.

"Even such rites as the autumn feasting could be transformed into harvest thanksgiving for God's goodness. Again, the missionaries were told not simply to import strange and inappropriate services from a foreign land. They were to provide services which were appropriately adapted for the English worshipers."

In emphasizing the need of adapting our presentations of the gospel as far as possible to the prevailing culture, Harris strongly urged that this should always be done without in any way compromising the gospel. But the principle behind converting heathen temples for Christian use could also be found in modern day England.

"We must adapt to each local culture," he said. "We have learned the value of gathered groups of Christians who witness to what we might call communities of common concern. For example, there are Christian youth organizations, seeker services, black majority churches and many other fellowships that have focused their witness on a particular group of people in a particular network of relationships or sub-culture. We need to do this if we are to reach people with the good news in words and images that they can understand.

"And what about the church plants that are successfully happening in secular buildings, in theaters, in pubs, because that's where the people meet and where they feel at home?" he asked the delegates. "That's where the Christians are going in order that they may form nuclei of worshipping believers."

Is the goal reachable?

Another pivotal question had to be answered at this second congress. Lynn Green posed it in one of his plenary sessions. "Now we're three years on," he said. "How does it look? Are we making progress? What does the overall picture look like?"

If they weren't making progress, if the goal looked unrealistic and unreachable, the fledgling movement would surely die an unmourned death.

"There does seem to be an upward trend," he informed the delegates. "Very careful investigation by Chris Forster and his team at Challenge 2000 indicate an increasing number of new churches planted in each five-year period beginning in 1975. Their very conservative analysis of less-than-complete data leads them to conclude that in these four periods there were at least 878, over 1,000, 1,162 and 1,559 new churches planted respectively.

"This is encouraging, but when you add it up you realize it is not sufficient to meet our goal. So is the 20/20 vision still realistic? Should we back off the goal of 20,000 new churches and 20 percent of the population attending church?"

Green had two basic answers to his questions.

"If we approach it from the point of view of need," he said, "then we couldn't do that. For instance, when you look at the number of churches per person and the number of people per church, you find that we really are at an almost all time low. As far back as mediaeval times around AD 1000 when church planting was so effective, there was a church for every 200 people. By 1851, this was down to one church for every 500 people and by 1989 one for every 1,200. We think that has just about turned around so that in 1995 we've eaten back by about 25 or 27 people for every church.

"Furthermore, even if we add 20,000 more churches, we still have to increase our average of 153 members per church in order to reach our goal of 20 percent of the population in regular attendance. In terms of need, at least 20,000 new churches is still a good goal."

Anticipating the 'exponential factor'

Green also talked about another way to look at the viability of the goal, what he called the "exponential factor." By way of illustration, he described the growth of the Alpha Courses developed by Sandy Miller, Vicar of the Anglican Holy Trinity Church in Brompton, London.

The Alpha Course, he says, is an evangelistic tool without parallel in his experience. Christians bring their unsaved friends for 13 weeks of small, informal dinner meetings. Each session includes a 20 minute presentation of some Bible truth. About 80 percent of all non-believers who attend come to know the Lord during that time.

The Alpha program started in 1974 with just four people. "By 1991 it had grown to 120 attending," Green explained, "but it had not multiplied. You are never going to reach a nation just by addition from four to 120."

By 1991, however, the course and method was so well developed that other churches began to take notice. As a result, it increased to 100 courses underway in just the next two years. In another two years it took a quantum leap to 1,000 churches using the course with 40,000 people attending each week!

"That's what I mean by exponential growth," said Green. "The new converts are the ones who bring their friends, 80 percent of whom will come to know the Lord. Those converts in turn bring their friends, so the numbers continue to multiply."

Rev. Miller has a real church-planting zeal for this outreach program. So far, five officially recognized parish churches have been planted and two of these have started daughter congregations.

"They could have started 35 or 40 new churches from this," explains Green, "but for the time being Miller wants to stay within the parish system. A great wave of new cell churches is the inevitable outcome of this exploding movement, however.

"This is just one indication that we are on the verge of a major church-planting movement in our country. There are others. But I believe that the Holy Spirit is able and indeed is demonstrating that he can inject an exponential factor into our DAWN movement. It is hard to predict how it will come, but when it does, I believe we'll be able to reach our goals.

"As we approach the 21st century and the end of our

time frame for this goal, we may need to extend the time. That's all right. That's what goals are for, so you can adjust as you go along. That's why we are meeting: to evaluate whether or not we are on target. It's probably too early now to extend that time frame. We can wait and see whether or not we are beginning something exponential.

"I don't believe we can back off the 20,000 churches or the 20 percent attending church. If it takes us an extra year or two or three or four, so be it. But it is a good goal to reach for."

A congress of 'enormous significance'

With many other speakers covering many other relevant topics in close to 40 seminars and plenary sessions, the Second DAWN England Congress came to a close. It seemed like every conceivable topic relating to evangelism and church planting in every possible setting and circumstance had been covered.

Steve Steele, our C.E.O., summarized all that he saw and heard from the view of one who is not an Englishman. "There was a great spirit of expectancy and revival in the air," he said. "It wouldn't surprise me at all if they actually increase their rate of growth and reach their goals."

The impact of the three days would also be felt in Scotland and Northern Ireland through the 35 or so delegates from those countries. Beyond that there was a profound sense that God was again anointing the Church in England to get back to its historic role as one of the leading missionary-sending nations of the world. It could return to its former colonies and other nations where its missionaries had pioneered with a new vision and strategy for this new day in missions.

God is in a hurry

In one plenary session of the Second Congress, Roger Forster detailed the growth history of the worldwide

Church from Pentecost to the present, and then likened the DAWN strategy of saturation church planting to "that lovely dragnet that Jesus spoke about concerning the Kingdom of God."

"The Kingdom of God is like a dragnet that covers the whole earth," he said. "It has no holes in it because each local church—full of the presence of God and full of the justice, joy and peace of the Kingdom—like a knot in the net, links up with the next church and the next church and the next church.

"Then the world will be netted, then the parable will reach its fulfillment, then Jesus will pull in the net to sort out the good and the bad, then Jesus will come again, then the new age will dawn upon us in its fullness.

"I believe that as this conference again carries this saturation church planting message into this country, we carry it further into the whole world."

Linking the DAWN strategy to this parable of our Lord, Roger again let his enthusiasm soar. To the cheers of these one thousand "staid" Englishmen, he concluded:

"Then the sun will not only be rising to dawn upon us but we will be in the place wherein the high noon and the loveliness of the Son of righteousness with healing in his wings will beam all over the regenerate human race in a new heaven and a new earth. That's where we're going, that's where we are pushing on. Let's get there as fast as possible. God is in a hurry because he said he is not slow concerning his promises. We are slow concerning his promises. He is running. And we want to run after him! Amen!"

Chapter Four

Understanding the DAWN Strategy

'My food,' said Jesus, 'is to do the will of him who sent me and to finish his work.'

John 4:34

I'll have to admit it came as an incredible yet very pleasant surprise to see evangelicals in England so exuberantly embrace the DAWN idea. DAWN had previously floundered in Canada and seemed light-years away from being adopted in the USA. It had been formulated in a third-world country and was being effectively transplanted into similar soils. But would it work in the sophisticated, powerful Church in the West?

The Church in England, as we saw in the last chapter, responds with a resounding "yes!"

Evangelical leaders have not only tightly grasped ownership of the vision and strategy but have developed the tactical aspects of the concept to a much deeper level as well. They are now teaching *us* what DAWN is all about and providing the model for reaching the rest of the Western world.

As a matter of fact, DAWN projects have now popped up with varying strengths and productivity in *every* nation of West Europe and the first projects are developing in Eastern Europe. Maybe the time is even coming when the

United States and Canada will catch the vision from across the sea!

DAWN as a specific kind of SCP project

Now that we have seen a DAWN project in action, I'd like to draw out from this England case study a systematic statement of the core idea of the strategy along with a description of the steps in the process that make it work. But first, some introductory comments.

At the heart of DAWN, as we have seen so far, is the concept of saturation church planting. It goes on from there to so integrate a number of basic components in synergistic fashion that a powerful system emerges.

The three models described in Chapter Two, by the way, focus on huge SCP goals of 62,500, 100,000 and 300,000 churches respectively. But though they connect or soon will connect with national DAWN projects, they are not DAWN projects in themselves.

As we have seen, an SCP project can be carried out at any level. A local church can draw a circle with a radius of, say, three kilometers around a section of a city or a group of villages and determine to saturate the area with churches. A denomination can do the same for a state, province or any size region.

Missionaries entering an unreached people group should develop a plan and strategy that will ultimately saturate that "nation" with churches. A group of churches or denominations can do this for a city, state or nation.

I am frequently asked, however, if a local church, denomination or city fellowship can develop a DAWN project. Technically, the answer is "no." DAWN works well because it is developed on a national scale based on a set of basic concepts that interact with each other in such a way as to develop a powerful synergism. Leave out one or more principles and you no longer are doing DAWN, Discipling A Whole *Nation*.

From our experience around the world we have learned that each of these ingredients and steps is essential to make the strategy work. One national project, for example, did everything but set a national goal for number of churches to be planted. Another emphasized major rallies and events rather than denominational programs. While there has been some good in these projects, they used a lot of human and financial resources without getting as much actual increase in overall growth rates as they could have.

As one leading business observer said, "DAWN is the most exciting movement God has raised up. It is powerful because it is an intentional process of amassing resources towards the right goal. Based on my background in business, everything makes sense. You cannot leave anything out of the process and still be effective."

Unlike many cooperative evangelical efforts, a DAWN-type project seeks to mobilize the whole Church of a nation to continuous action over a period of many years. It calls for a permanent paradigm shift in the way local churches, denominations and missions do ministry.

We frequently refer to such projects, by the way, as DAWN-*type* strategies. That is, they embody all the basic elements of a DAWN strategy including the core idea of SCP, of saturation church planting. But they might appear under any number of different banners, be sponsored by any one of existing or *ad hoc* agencies, take on any variety of culturally appropriate tactics and have much or little connection with Dawn Ministries as an organization. In the last chapter, for example, we saw that an *ad hoc* committee formed and developed the structure called "Challenge 2000." This organization in turn adopted the DAWN *strategy* and held DAWN *congresses*.

The core idea of DAWN

Knowing this book will be read by many who are encountering the DAWN vision for the first time, my temptation is to describe in great detail and with many good illustrations the full DAWN process. For one concern we have in Dawn Ministries is that some will see the simplicity of the DAWN strategy and begin a project before they also understand the depth of each aspect of the process. For the sake of the many others who are already immersed in the DAWN movement, I will restrain myself here and instead encourage the reading or re-reading of *DAWN 2000.*

As explained in detail in that book, the core idea of the DAWN strategy for world evangelization goes like this:[1]

> DAWN aims at mobilizing the whole Body of Christ in whole countries in a determined effort to complete the Great Commission in that country by working toward the goal of providing an evangelical congregation for every village and neighborhood of every class, kind and condition of people in the whole country.
>
> It is concerned that Jesus Christ become incarnate in all his beauty, compassion, power and message in the midst of every small group of people—400 or so to 1,000 or more in number—in a whole country including all its "reached" and "unreached" people groups.
>
> When this is accomplished, it is not assumed the Great Commission for a country has been completed, but that a practical and measurable goal has been reached toward making a disciple of that country and all the "nations" within it.
>
> With a witnessing congregation in every small community of people, it is now possible to communicate the gospel in the most direct, contextualized and productive way to every person in that land.
>
> Every person now has a reasonable opportunity to make an informed, intelligent decision for or against

the Lord Jesus Christ.

Everyone now has a church within easy access both in a practical as well as cultural sense where he or she can attend and be further trained in discipleship should he or she become a believer.

The penultimate (next to last) step for making a disciple of every "nation" in a country has been reached.

When this happens in *every* country in the world, we can almost hear the trumpet sound. The primary task the Lord gave his Church is close to completion and the Lord can soon return for his bride.

Of all the many affirmations of this DAWN strategy we have heard from around the world, I still like best the comment of a former Methodist bishop in Zimbabwe. "DAWN is a one-word summary of the Great Commission," he said to Dawn missionary Ted Olsen. "Jesus told his followers to make disciples of all nations. DAWN is the essence of our Lord's command."

Describing the principles and process

To speak of the specific principles of DAWN, to start with, can be a bit misleading. In the last book, for instance, I broke the concepts down into a list of 12. Some added prayer as a 13th item, certainly something that should permeate every aspect of the DAWN process whether listed separately or not.

Sometimes we have spoken of the three basic pillars of DAWN being the saturation church planting strategy, the research process and the intercessory foundation. We then refer to other facets of the strategy as corollaries or supporting activities.

In preparing an article for those involved in the AD2000 and Beyond Movement, I wrote that a true DAWN project—sometimes called a DAWN-type project—is a saturation church planting process carried out at a national level and includes eight steps and ingredients. For each item I gave a thumb-nail sketch of a national leader who particularly exemplified that particular aspect of the strategy. This composite I referred to as the ideal DAWN strategy.

With some modifications and amplifications, the description of the ideal DAWN project is repeated here.

1. ***It is a DAWN project if*** there is a national leader and a national committee with a firm resolve and commitment to work at mobilizing the whole Body of Christ in a whole nation in a long-term repeating strategy that leads most directly to the discipling of the nation including all the people groups within it. Such a leader, along with the national committee, is sometimes referred to as a "John Knoxer," a man or woman or small group who embody the prayer of the reformer in Scotland whose life-long cry was "Give me my country or I die."

This leader must not only have the passion and calling but also the spiritual gifts, the experience, the respect of national Church leaders and, significantly, the organizational structure necessary for mobilizing the Church of a nation in a DAWN project.[2]

As DAWN has developed around the world, we have seen an honor roll of such godly men and women rise to the occasion. At least one DAWN project leader has been martyred as a direct result of his role in the growth of the evangelical church in his nation.

Others have risked jail, sold their homes, left their jobs and otherwise sacrificed their security and tranquillity in order to be involved at some level of the process of filling their country with congregations of new converts.

These godly men and women have emerged to take up the cause of the discipling of their nation under a great range of circumstances. The size, strength and spiritual dynamic of the Church varies from place to place. Likewise, the receptivity to the gospel or the degree of repression and persecution is different in each situation. For these creative and persistent leaders, however, a way is usually found to keep the movement alive.

In 1986, Dawn Ministries was still in its infancy, functioning out of one bedroom in our small tract home in San Jose, California, when **Kari and Terttu Törmä** rang our door bell. They were on their way from Finland to attend the World Vision Board meeting, of which Kari was a member, in Southern California.

With tears streaming down their faces, they told their story.

"There are scars on our bodies from attempts to develop evangelistic programs for discipling our nation," Kari said to my wife Lyn and me. "We have followed the DAWN idea through your writings for 15 years. If this isn't the answer for Finland, we don't know where else to turn."

As we listened, we understood a little of the difficulty. "The only people in the world harder to reach than Finns are Muslims," Kari told us. "We are a close, introspective, introverted people. We were used by the rulers of Sweden for 800 years, then by the Russians up to the Bolshevik revolution.

"Our winters are hard. The ice age scraped all the good soil off the top. Peasants barely eke out a living. All of this produces a mistrust for any but a very close circle of friends and relatives."

Kari went on to tell us of the discouraging religious climate. "Finland has a state church, Lutheran, to which 86.5 percent of the people belong. Only a tiny handful, however, are truly evangelical. It is hard to get the Lutheran Church interested in evangelism, and perhaps even harder to plant churches other than Lutheran."

When we met Kari again in 1987 at our international John Knox conference in London, a group of us laid hands on him and prayed that Satan would be defeated in his desire to keep the gospel from spreading throughout that land. Kari later testified that he had been in deep depression for seven years. "Since your prayer," he told us, "God has lifted the depression and increased my faith."

It would be still more years, however, before we would see the Church of Finland come together in unity and commitment to make a disciple of their homeland. Mark the dates of November 17 to 20, 1994, when a DAWN Congress was finally held. That's when it happened!

"There was a major miracle and incredible breakthrough," reports Wolfgang Fernández, our coordinator for Europe. "We were just overwhelmed with the marvelous way God used our teammates there. The response was beyond our dreams."

What was the response? In the first place, a larger-than-expected group of 220 leaders came, enthusiastically embraced the vision and committed themselves to reach their nation for Christ.

The wildest hope was that the delegates might set an overall goal of 400 to 500 new congregations. Instead, they boldly committed themselves to start 2,000 new churches by the year 2000! The *Lutherans* set a goal to plant 1,400 churches! After years of darkness for the Church of Finland, dawn had arrived and DAWN had arrived. It could not have happened, however, without a man who truly was giving his life for this vision.

2. ***It is a DAWN project if*** it is built on the premise that the most direct way to work at the discipling of a whole nation is to fill it with evangelical congregations so that there is one within easy access both practically and culturally of every person of every class, kind and condition of mankind in that nation. This includes all "reached" and "unreached" people groups.

Sometimes such people groups are obvious as when you are dealing with the Muslims in northern Ghana. Sometimes it is harder to recognize them such as when these same Muslim people are gathered in little neighborhoods in the cities in the South. Actually, research indicates there are as many hidden in the southern cities as there are in the villages of the North, and are more responsive to the gospel in the cities!

Unchurched and unsaved white, Anglo-Saxon Protestants can even be hidden in some obvious places. DAWN researchers in England, for example, found little towns within reach of a parish church that were being overlooked. Such little villages might have three or four buildings servicing ten or 20 farms. These folk with traditional values were interested in the gospel, but were without transportation—or interest—in going any distance to a church. The solution in this case was to begin to develop congregations in the only social gathering places in their little communities: the local pubs.

In every city, in every nation, there are untold numbers of unchurched segments of society, whether they would fit the technical definition of "unreached" or not.

For sheer dogged determination and persistence in communicating this vision year after year for two whole decades, there is none yet like **Jun Balayo** of the Philippines. Through the early years in the 1970's when the idea of filling a nation with evangelical congregations was new to the Philippines—let alone the rest of the world—Jun remained steadfast.

Against many odds, he labored in just one region of the nation. He brought a bright and dedicated team together. They held hundreds of local seminars and persisted in research and communicating their findings in an excellent monthly publication.

The result was that many denominations and thousands of local congregations had the vision constantly held before them and were given many tools to carry it out. Ultimately, DAWN 2000 Philippines flourished throughout the whole nation, and as of this writing, is preparing for its sixth national DAWN Congress.

3. ***It is a DAWN project if*** there has been adequate research that determines:

a) the number of denominations in a country,

b) their respective number of local churches and members and/or average attendance,

c) the average annual growth rates (AAGR's) of each denomination,

d) the methodologies being used by various groups that are producing the best growth,

e) the ratio of churches to population for the whole nation and for every sub-group of the nation, and

f) such contextual factors as the history, economy, religion, culture, politics, natural disasters and other societal forces that tend to indicate the relative responsiveness of the population and the methodologies and themes that might best see a response to the gospel.

I'm tempted to write at length concerning this matter of research. It is so crucial to a successful national strategy. It is absolutely foundational. It is what I referred to in *DAWN 2000* as the first component among equals.

For one thing, having this kind of data is always of interest to Church leaders. They will come to a meeting to get such information. For another, it is the hard, cold facts that time and again have motivated the Church in a nation to action. It is what we call the "Nehemiah effect." Nehemiah was a man who gave up his cushy job, risked his life and then undertook the almost impossible task of arousing a complacent, defeated nation to action. With incredible zeal, persistence and fortitude, he kept the people at work until the wall was finished.

What was the motivating factor? It all began when he got the data about his home city and nation. The information drove him to undertake this huge task at considerable risk to himself. We have seen this same kind of transformation in attitude in nation after nation as the facts of the Church and nation are presented.

A second reason for wanting to write further about research is that it is perhaps the most difficult, and misunderstood aspect of a DAWN project. Our Church leaders are not trained in Bible school and seminary for this kind of activity. In some cultures it is a rather foreign concept.

For those who supervise or do the research for a DAWN project, we suggest reading the relevant chapters in the *DAWN 2000* book, the *DAWN Research Handbook* by Roy Wingerd and, as soon as it comes out, the new book by Wingerd and Steve Spaulding entitled: *Joshua Handbook: Seeing With a View To What Must Be Done.* These will all be available from Dawn Ministries.

Xolisani Dlamini of Zimbabwe is representative of that special breed that, in some circumstances at least, risks life and limb to get the data needed for a successful DAWN project.

In completing the research for one region of Zimbabwe, Xolisani hiked hundreds of kilometers, wore out five pair of shoes, interviewed scores of Church leaders and spoke with dozens of government officials. In the process he encountered lions, deadly cobras, angry elephants and even killers wielding machetes and witches breathing satanic curses.

But even more important, Xolisani helped gather the data that led the participants in a DAWN Congress to set a goal of planting 10,000 more churches, a goal that many are successfully working towards.

On completion of his first round of data gathering, Xolisani said, "Now I know that the research I undertook was a divine appointment. Research is a most important thing! Without it, we simply will not know how strong or how weak the church is or where we need to plant new churches."

Or, as Ross Campbell, now with the AD2000 Movement, said after their first round of research in Ghana,

"Nothing was the way we imagined it. We have had to change our whole strategy for 'churching' this country."

4. ***It is a DAWN project if*** a national congress is held where the primary leaders of all denominations and other parachurch organizations along with leading pastors gather to consider the discipling of their whole nation and analyze the data that has been collected.

This is, obviously, the most visible aspect of a DAWN-type project. It is the event where anywhere from 50 to 1,500 delegates representing every stripe of evangelical are gathered in unity and commitment to a long-range strategy of working towards a common goal.

Putting together such a congress requires great persistence in finding and gathering just the right mix of leaders, brilliance and spiritual insight in developing the prophetic message and a program to communicate it, skill in gathering and supervising a strong team of workers, ability to cut costs and raise large amounts of money—and much more! Committees are needed for selection of delegates, finances, site selection and arrangements, housing of delegates, congress program, communications and so on.

Tom Houston, formerly International Director for the Lausanne Committee for World Evangelization, warns that it will be disastrous "...to move ahead before the whole Body is ready." The unity of the Church in some countries makes it possible to start a project almost as soon as it is presented. In Finland it took eight years before such unity came. In Japan, at this writing, there is such division between Pentecostals and non-Pentecostals that the time is still not ripe for a true DAWN project.

Sometimes there is need for a major spiritual breakthrough. Such was the case in Argentina in September 1994, when leaders were gathered for an initial meeting to consider whether to proceed with a DAWN project or not. Bob Smart, who first experienced DAWN in his native England, broke down all barriers with his humble approach.

"I come in the name of the English Church to apologize for what my country did in the Falklands war," he said. "I confess also the pride that we as a Church felt."

At this point, Dawn missionary Berna Salcedo heard someone cry. It turned out to be one of the pastors who had participated in that hostility. Soon other pastors were weeping all around the room. Someone asked Alberto De Luca, leader of the meeting, to give brother Smart a hug as a sign of forgiveness. From that point on, it was not difficult for the Church to come together for a DAWN Congress and national strategy.

Israel Brito of the Dominican Republic is one whose dedication to bringing the Church together for a national strategy resulted in a triumphant congress. He returned home from a DAWN training seminar in Florida at a time when churches were disappearing, but with a great vision to saturate his country with Christ-centered congregations.

Mortgaging his house to raise the initial $25,000 and gathering a strong team around him, Brito succeeded in bringing together in a DAWN Congress 3,000 leaders that represented virtually every local congregation in the nation. They in turn set a goal and are working effectively at planting churches in each of 5,000 unchurched villages and neighborhoods.

In some countries, of course, it is impossible to have a public congress like this. Some have therefore concluded it was impossible to have a DAWN project in "closed" nations or in nations with only a handful of believers. But Dawn Missionary Roy Wingerd, who oversees our work in East Asia, refutes this notion. "The purpose of a congress is to bring about unity and consensus on a strategy for the discipling of a nation," he says. "You can accomplish this purpose by meeting individually with leaders all over a nation. You can have a 'one-by-one' or 'two-by-two' congress. You need consensus, not just a meeting."

5. ***It is a DAWN project if*** the delegation gathered at the national congress collectively commits itself to a specific number of churches to be planted by a specific date. This goal can either be suggested by the national committee based on the research done or can be the collective goal of all the denominations, missions and other parachurch organizations. (See next point.)

One of the best ways to set a national church-planting goal—and get commitment to it by all denominations in a country—is the way they did it in England.

As we saw in Chapter Three, the national Challenge 2000 (DAWN) committee spent many hours praying and poring over the data that had been gathered through their research project. They concluded that a goal of 20,000 new churches by AD 2000 seemed to be what the Spirit was saying.

But they shared this goal with no one. Instead, they had each denomination set their own goals at the Congress held in February, 1993. When these individual goals were added together, the total came to almost exactly 20,000!

It was great confirmation to all that this represented the mind of Christ. With this conviction, the multiplication of churches throughout England is overcoming many years of decline.

6. ***It is a DAWN project if*** each evangelical denomination, mission agency and other group sets its own goals for number of churches to be planted by a certain date and develops and implements plans to reach that goal. It is expected that all parachurch organizations that do not plant churches themselves will so orient their ministries that they truly work "alongside" churches and denominations in their church-multiplication projects.

All the activities of a DAWN process are useless if the participants do not make specific commitments to national and organizational goals for massive church-planting efforts. For example, a brilliant study[3] of the status of the Churches in Canada was prepared for their National Leadership Consultation on Evangelism sponsored by the Vision 2000 Canada organization in May 1990. It clearly demonstrated an immediate need for 6,700 new congregations split almost evenly between French-speaking and English-speaking sections of the country.

At the congress, however, there was no such national goal set. Informal reports indicate that while a few denominations developed their own goals and plans, the overall result in growth of the Church in Canada has been negligible.

The case of Guatemala, however, gives another picture. Though there was general consensus that the Church should work towards becoming 50 percent of the population by 1990 through doubling their 7,000 churches, they did not actually set a specific goal at the Congress in 1984. Among other things, they were hesitant to throw this in the face of the dominant Roman Catholic Church. Furthermore, the national DAWN committee took little leadership in continuing the movement for years after the Congress. (As this is being written, a new national committee is being formed and another national Congress planned.)

Still, 15 individual denominations did set goals and developed plans for church-multiplication efforts. Under such names as "Vision 90," "Faith Projection," "Advance," "One by One by One," and so on, goals were set to double or triple their number of churches, have each church start a new church or reach a total of 1,000 churches. Most of these were five-year goals.

These individual denominational efforts kept a growth movement alive without a national focus and strong committee. Effective denominational projects of this nature include the same components as the national DAWN project.

Adonai Leiva, DAWN project leader and head of Campus Crusade in El Salvador, saw the value of such denominational projects from the beginning. In their first Amanecer (DAWN) Congress in 1987, Leiva encouraged all 55 participating denominations to establish measurable, challenging, yet reachable goals. If they would increase churches by 12 percent a year, evangelicals could become 30 percent of the population by 1990.

Adonai mobilized his own team to work alongside denominations in this process. When a peace treaty was later signed after 12 years of war, Leiva so encouraged all denominations that now there are churches even in the heart of the former guerrilla territory!

7. ***It is a DAWN project if*** there is a national committee formed to keep the movement alive

a) through continued data gathering by means of a permanent national research function,

b) through a publication that reports on the exciting growth and challenging aspects of each denominational program,

c) through seminars and consultations with denominational leaders and pastors in various regions and

d) through planning for the next national congress where evaluation is made of progress to date and new plans and goals set for the future.

Sometimes God even uses a foreign missionary to take strong leadership in a DAWN-type project. Such is the case of Swiss missionary **Werner Spalinger** who has faced the same risks as all pastors and national leaders in the violence of Peru. The committee God led him to bring together first held a fantastic DAWN Congress, called "Peru for Christ," that resulted in around 1,000 pastors setting a goal to start 40,000 new churches.

But what happens after goals are set and the congress is over?

What needs to be done is what Spalinger helped the

national committee to do. They are continuing the research to determine what is happening. They are publishing a national magazine so everyone can see what progress is being made and what still needs to be done. Perhaps most significantly, they are holding six regional congresses to infuse the vision into the 10,000 pastors of the nation.

With this kind of follow-up, they will be ready to repeat the DAWN cycle and hold another congress in due time. They will keep the saturation church planting vision alive, Lord willing, until the Lord Himself interrupts with his shout of triumph to gather all his saints to be with him forever.

8. ***It will be a truly powerful DAWN project if*** it is undergirded by effective prayer movements on national, regional, denominational and local church levels.

As the current proliferation of books on world revival emphasize, prayer is the key. "The evangelical scholar J. Edwin Orr," writes David Bryant,[4] "summarized into one simple statement his sixty years of historical study on great prayer movements preceding major spiritual awakenings: *'Whenever God is ready to do something new with his people, he always sets them to praying.'*"

If God indeed is "about to do something new" in mobilizing his Body in nation after nation and in the whole world to complete his 2,000-year-old command, surely this also will come about as he sets us to praying.

Where would we be without intercessors like **Jean Lim**?

God raised her up from a family of idol worshippers in Indonesia and from a life of gambling and greed. She came through a series of deaths of loved ones, attempted suicides, enslavement to Japanese Buddhism and attendance with mediums and witch doctors.

"Now," she says, "I just love to pray and wait upon the Lord in His presence for hours and hours."

God has also used her to lead one of the most powerful prayer ministries connected with any DAWN project in the world. Her extended times of intercession, her small prayer group, her constant travels around the nation to organize prayer cells and her organizing of special seasons of prayer all mightily empower the Malaysia DAWN vision of planting 4,000 new churches.

I think there are two sides of the prayer coin that need equal emphasis. One is the spiritual warfare aspect of breaking down strongholds of the enemy in individuals, in cities, in people groups, in nations or wherever they occur. When satanic forces are bound or scattered, there is then entrance for the gospel. This, rightfully, is receiving a lot of attention and is another indication of the world-wide revival we are in. It is a significant factor in being able to complete the Great Commission in our time.

The other side of the coin is prayer for revival. It is still the cry of the Lord that "...if *my* people, who are called by my name, will humble themselves and pray and seek my face and turn from their wicked ways, *then* will I hear from heaven and will forgive their sin and will heal their land" (II Chron. 7:14).

DAWN breaking around the world

With the England model as a reference point and the above as a summary statement of the DAWN strategy, we can now move on to see how national leaders in Africa feel about it, how DAWN fits in with the unreached peoples movement, how DAWN has been embraced by a whole region with a view to the rest of the world and finally how the DAWN vision might ultimately take root even in North America. These are the topics to be covered in Part II.

---

[1] From *DAWN 2000: 7 Million Churches to Go*, pp. 12, 13.

[2] The role and function of the "John Knoxer" is further explained in *DAWN 2000*, pp. 9-10, 91-94, 176-180, 187-196.

[3] Arnell Motz, editor, *Reclaiming a Nation* (Richmond, B.C., Canada: Church Leadership Library, 1990).

[4] David Bryant, *The Hope At Hand* (Grand Rapids, MI: Baker Books, 1995), pp. 30, 31.

Part II

DAWN Around the World

Chapter Five

Zimbabwe: The Challenge of Africa

'Political dreams have turned into nightmares. People are facing real pressures and looking for real answers.'

Ngwiza Mnkandla
Pastor in Zimbabwe

Several years ago, a skeptic posed this riddle to Ted Olsen, Dawn Ministries' Regional Coordinator for Africa: "How is the DAWN strategy similar to a dinosaur? Answer: It starts with the letter 'd' and soon will also be extinct."

"Critics have said DAWN won't work in Africa because nations are too large, people groups too diverse and the Church too fragmented," says Olsen. "Yet, the Discipling A Whole Nation vision has weathered this critical onslaught in Africa and survived."

The challenges, nonetheless, have been real. There were discouraging factors within the African context, great weaknesses in much of the Church and adjustments that had to be made in the implementation of DAWN itself. I consider it remarkable that the strategy has taken such deep root in Zimbabwe and begun its spread to other nations.

To tell this story of the emergence and acceptance of DAWN in Africa, I will introduce you to four key people. One is Ted Olsen, the other three are Zimbabwean Church leaders who caught the vision and turned it into reality.

Ted Olsen, Missionary Kid

"In the school of logic and common sense," Olsen says, "I might never have chosen Zimbabwe as a launching pad for DAWN in sub-Equatorial Africa. Other than having gathered some general information on factors relating to receptivity, the growth of the Church and the socio-political climate, I had no intellectual reason for making this my starting point."

Not that Olsen was a stranger to Africa. He grew up here as the son of missionary parents. His father had a prolific ministry in evangelism and church planting among blacks, coloreds (mixed breeds) and Indians. Olsen went through the South African school system, graduated from one of their best universities, served as an investigative reporter for the Cape Town Times for ten years and married Judy Owen-Johnston, a South African girl of English extraction. In 1980 the Lord led them for the first time to move as a family to America.

"We might have spent the rest of our lives there had we not met Jim Montgomery," Olsen testifies. "Learning of my background, he encouraged me to join his staff in the Research and Strategy Department of Overseas Crusades, now OC International. It wasn't long before the DAWN vision became deeply and forever my own. Even after Jim left OC to start Dawn Ministries in 1985, we continued to work together."

Zimbabwe burning brightly

So it was that Ted and I came to be in Zimbabwe on a fact-finding mission in the early part of 1985. Almost never has a DAWN project been started in a country unless there was an invitation from some national leaders to do so. Ted and I, however, hit Zimbabwe cold and simply began calling pastors and leaders whose names we found in the phone book in Harare, the capital.

"What actually drew me there," Ted says, "was an almost surreal experience of looking at a map of Africa. It was as if Zimbabwe were alight, burning brightly out of the heart of the continent. I couldn't help but conclude this was God's way of telling me this was the nation from which DAWN would take off in Africa."

That first ground-breaking trip to Zimbabwe lasted a marathon six weeks. At the end of this time, Ted called a meeting for denominational leaders in a Harare hotel. The 50 or so who attended represented a wide spectrum of churches. After a three-hour presentation of DAWN including a lot of details gathered during the preceding weeks, he asked the all-important question: "Do you think it's time for the Church to unite behind a whole-nation DAWN thrust?" When he asked for a response, every leader in the room, without exception, put up his or her hand.

At that time, Olsen was not serving with Dawn Ministries nor was he resident in Africa. So all he could do was leave behind a lot of good intentions and strong encouragement. It was several months before he was able to return, renew relationships and continue the research in preparation for the initial consultation.

From his long experience, Ted realized that in Africa nothing gets off the ground unless it's forged through relationships. Knowing someone and feeling a bond of trust and camaraderie is paramount to getting any kind of job done. It therefore took him many months of meeting leaders, talking with them on the phone, finding out about their lives, their ministry and their families before he got to first base in developing DAWN.

From there, DAWN developed along lines similar to other projects around the world, but with a distinct African pace and flavor. Without national ownership of DAWN, it never really gets off the ground. In this case, it was Roy Jacobs, a white native of Zimbabwe, who took leadership in bringing about 300 church leaders for an initial consultation in April, 1987. Jacobs, who has since gone to be with the Lord, was successful also in bringing several leaders from South Africa, Malawi, Zambia and even some from communist Mozambique.

Though this was not a full-scale DAWN congress, still the denomination leaders that were present set individual goals that added up to more than 2,000 new churches within the next decade. This was not spectacular, but it did serve as a booster rocket to what DAWN would become in the ensuing years. The point that God wanted to build his Church was well made and well taken. Helping the process along was Dr. C. Peter Wagner, who served as the main plenary speaker and urged commitment to the DAWN vision and strategy.

Later that year, OC sent the Olsen family back to Africa with a team of missionaries to help bolster the process. Because of visa restrictions in Zimbabwe, they located in nearby Swaziland. The plan was to work closely with the national committee in developing and implementing the national strategy, beginning with research.

As the data soon began to bear out, the larger evangelical and mainline denominations were not necessarily getting larger. The drawn-out civil war, which ended just prior to independence in 1980, had taken a serious toll on the growth of these churches. Urban church leaders had been cut off from congregations in war-torn rural regions for long periods. Churches had died by the hundreds. Intimidation by Marxist freedom fighters drove nominal Christians out of fellowship. Many churches were literally obliterated and thousands of believers who stood true to Christ were killed.

Now, eight years after independence, DAWN appeared on the scene. The key researcher, a Zimbabwean by the name of Xolisani Dlamini, who was trained by Roy Wingerd, another Dawn missionary, became a major resource as God worked in his life and gave him a strong prophetic voice which was heard across the nation at one DAWN consultation after another. An able national committee helped plan and execute these regional meetings in the five major centers within the space of two years. This prepared the way for a full DAWN Congress in 1989.

By 1992, the Church in the nation had heard the DAWN vision. Ngwiza Mnkandla, a national leader, estimates that possibly 80 percent of the evangelical pastors and leaders had taken note of DAWN. The next logical step for DAWN in Zimbabwe was another national congress, which took place at the University of Zimbabwe, Harare, in September of 1992. This consultation, called TARGET 2000, lasted a week and drew over 500 delegates. Nothing before in the history of the Church in that nation had so successfully drawn leaders together from across denominational lines in one place at one time to focus on one particular challenge.

Findings from the excellent research document that was presented, case studies from far and wide and a resounding prophetic message made this a truly unique moment in the life of the Church. A national goal of 10,000 new churches by the year 2000 was set and a national DAWN committee was affirmed to keep this vision alive.

Subsequent research uncovered at least 3,400 new churches established in the following three years with an estimated 1,639,760 converts incorporated. Their plan for the next 12 months was to hold DAWN-type conferences in 16 regions of the nation. The Target 2000 committee felt this would further speed the growth of the Church as the vision was cast at a more grass-roots level.

Come 1999, a final consultation will be held and, things continuing as they are, will be a time of great triumph and celebration as the progress toward the goal is reviewed. Anticipation is high that it will not only be met, but will be surpassed.

To get the flavor of DAWN in Africa, however, you need to interact with the national leaders who are giving their lives to it. Therefore, I asked Olsen to interview his closest national associates. In response, he sent me a sketch of three key leaders and an audio tape of his interviews

Ngwiza Mnkandla: a reluctant convert

For a few years in the mid-80's, Ngwiza Mnkandla, Director of Faith Ministries in Harare, was on the fringes of the DAWN movement. Although he did not attend the 1987 consultation, he heard plenty about the vision and purpose of DAWN. Many of his colleagues in ministry across the nation could talk about little else. Still, his desire was to build and lead a big church—possibly the biggest—in the capital city of Harare.

It was not until 1989 when he came across a copy of the book, *DAWN 2000: 7 Million Churches to Go*, that the whole-nation strategy of saturation church planting began to make sense.

About this time, one of his lay leaders in Faith Ministries had been struck by the words in Acts 5:28. He noted that the charge brought by the high priest against the apostles was that they had filled Jerusalem with their doctrine. Leaders at Faith Ministries agreed this had prophetic significance for them: they were to fill Harare with their doctrine through the planting of churches. This was a major shift away from "big mono-campus" thinking toward the church multiplication mindset.

Since that critical moment in 1989, Ngwiza has been a key figure in the development of DAWN in Zimbabwe and has shared the vision in other nations of Africa as well.

Freddie Gwanzura: inflamed by DAWN

We met pastor Freddie Gwanzura in Chapter Two. Gwanzura left his building contractor's business in 1976 and became a full-time worker with the Apostolic Faith

Mission (AFM) Church in the Masvingo region of Zimbabwe. Soon he was pastoring a congregation of 60 in the Macheke township on the outskirts of the town. Later, he became Provincial Overseer for AFM.

By the time Freddie was introduced to the DAWN vision, he had just a few churches in his region, though he wasn't sure how many. "That was before DAWN," he says. "Previously, I had no idea of the scope of my 'parish'—the Province of Masvingo. I was not moved by its enormity nor the number of lost in my own backyard. It was the emphasis on gathering good information and developing a plan of operation based on this information that really challenged me," he says.

Today, Freddie now has 21 church leaders and over 200 churches under his supervision. DAWN thinking is now at the heart of his work. "This is the vision that possesses me," he says. "Planting new congregations in all the villages and growth points in our province is the main thing God wants us to do."

Richmond Chiundiza: In trouble with the Fire Marshall

From the beginning, Richmond Chiundiza has been one of the prime movers in getting DAWN started in Zimbabwe and other African nations as well, though he also had a big-church mentality.

In 1987, he rented a cinema which was soon packed with 700 people. The local Fire Marshall didn't like that at all and threatened to close down the congregation if they had even one too many people crowded into the building.

Chiundiza's solution was to send 100 of his congregation off to start another church. Soon the cinema was again filled to overflowing and Richmond had to send out another 100. This was repeated until now there are 11 daughter congregations of this one local church!

Chiundiza's Glad Tidings Fellowship then set a goal to

reach 67 total churches that would cover all major urban centers of Zimbabwe in the year 1995 and then multiply congregations in rural areas throughout the nation beginning in 1996.

DAWN through their eyes

"When Jim Montgomery phoned me from Colorado Springs to help him with this chapter," Ted writes, "my first thought was to interview these three men who are John Knoxers in the finest sense." Though Olsen recorded an interview with each of them separately, I have combined and slightly edited their responses to his questions.

Ted: The readiness of the Church for a DAWN project as well as the size of the goal it will set depends to a certain extent on how responsive the people are to the gospel. What is your understanding and experience relating to this matter of receptivity?

Ngwiza: Receptivity is very high. Political dreams have turned into nightmares. Leaders who came to power promising the earth have failed miserably. The socio-economic situation which was at the heart of the political promises is subsequently a wasteland. Africa is catching up with the frustrations and traumas of industrialized nations in the rest of the world. People are facing real pressures and are looking for real answers. Life has become a struggle to survive.

People need to have something to give them hope. Africa is very ripe for the gospel; the level of receptiveness is extremely high. As a result, growth in the church is explosive in many areas. The potential for planting churches far and wide is incredible. Those of us in Church leadership must change our thinking, our leadership styles and our structures in the church to accommodate what's going on. We cannot contain this new wine in old wineskins.

Richmond: I am shocked every week by the number of people coming to Christ. This past Sunday, I was preaching in our city center church and 45 people accepted Christ. I went from there to another of our services in a high-density area. Another 60 people accepted Christ. At still another of our congregations our Sunday morning service drew so many people we had to take every available chair into the yard outside. Again, dozens came to Christ. I'm seeing this all the time. In our Glad Tidings Fellowship, we now have 43 congregations throughout the country that are averaging 50 conversions per Sunday. That's about 2,000 new converts a week in just our new, little fellowship.

The problem in the Church as a whole is that our leaders are blind to this receptivity factor. The pace of growth from new conversions is subsequently too slow. If the churches could understand the hunger that is there, we would stop playing our little games. Anyone who preaches the straight gospel without any additives will be shocked by the response. The simple message that 'God loves me' brings people into the Kingdom.

Ted: When you think back to the mid-1980's when the DAWN vision was first shared in Zimbabwe, what was it that captured your imagination?

Ngwiza: Nehemiah was one of the key factors in my life. As I read the Nehemiah story and encountered the DAWN vision for the first time, some quickening was taking place in my heart. Back then, we were trying to rebuild the Evangelical Fellowship of Zimbabwe (EFZ), which was pretty much in ruins. We were not doing anything together. It was clearly time to rebuild the walls of our Fellowship, but we were lacking unity.

When the vision of DAWN came in, I saw we could bring unity in the Body behind this wonderful goal. Obviously, a lot has happened since that time. On the national level, DAWN is the focus of our thinking. We're not going to set it aside.

In terms of my own ministry, the DAWN vision is our main focus in Faith Ministries. In 1992 when we had the Target 2000 DAWN Congress here in Harare, we had only six congregations. In just three years we've grown to 25. We are constantly reminding ourselves that we are committed to a total of 40 new churches by the year 2000. We are coming up with radical decisions in terms of how we're operating and what changes we need to make in our strategy in order to reach this goal.

Richmond: The idea behind DAWN—that the presence of Christ should be planted within easy reach of every person in a nation—was a wonderful vision that challenged me personally. When DAWN brought in the whole country approach, I thought: This is it! The vision for reaching the nation has been analyzed, defined and laid out. How could we not embrace it? How could we not involve ourselves with this strategy?

I had been involved in evangelistic crusades and other ways of reaching the lost. But I knew in my heart there must be a better way. When I heard the DAWN challenge, it confirmed what was already developing in my heart.

One thing I like about DAWN is that it did not come with an agenda. Some people come to Zimbabwe and say: "This is the best method in the world to accomplish the task and here is an outline of the steps you need to take." I don't like that approach. I feel trapped in a corner. DAWN helps us catch the vision but does not attempt to dictate things which are really contextual. DAWN helps us define and aim at the goal. Now I sit down with other leaders who share this commitment of saturating our nation with churches. We become creative and figure out how best to do it. In the end, DAWN is the common denominator that brings unity.

Another thing that impressed me about DAWN was that I could see it was biblical. The apostles proclaimed the gospel, then brought together those who believed into churches. This is what DAWN embodies. When I understood this, I realized this was the strategy for our nation.

Ted: Though there is much freedom to develop DAWN

according to practical realities, the one thing DAWN does emphasize is the multiplication of new churches. How does this fit the African situation?

Richmond: I understand this issue in two different ways. For one, there is the gifting part. Spiritual gifts are given to African believers just like all others. People who are gifted to start new ministry—in this case, new churches—respond in a practical, deliberate way. There is no problem here.

Then there is the more spontaneous reality. As we share the challenge for planting churches, some people catch the vision who do not necessarily have the apostolic gifting.

Many people in our depressed economy, for example, have had to go back to their rural homes where they can afford to live. Particularly when they've had the training in church planting that we offer in the city church, they start winning souls and pulling people together in fellowship. A new church will get started in this way. This is happening often in Zimbabwe.

I see this model in the Bible. Many New Testament churches were planted where the apostles had never been. These churches were started as a result of the persecution and dispersion. Suddenly there were churches everywhere. In present-day Africa, such a phenomenon is fanned into a flame in a nation when DAWN is present and in some stage of implementation.

Freddie: Church planting is the best method of outreach in Africa. It really works. If 15 people accept Christ in an evangelistic outreach, you will have 15 people in church the next time you call a meeting. Someone immediately takes responsibility for them. This man will be the person who follows through on these converts and attends to their continued growth. He becomes the pastor of this new flock. He disciples them and sends them out to win other souls immediately.

In this way, there is a built-in capacity to see this

church start another church in the near future. This is how we are reaching our province—through starting new congregations through evangelistic outreach. Thanks to the DAWN vision, we have been able to develop a plan and implement it on a scale which we feel is at the heart of the Great Commission.

***Ted:* Is a power encounter a significant factor in planting churches in villages where Jesus has never before been preached?**

Freddie: Africa is dominated by ancestral spirits. The power of the demons behind these spirits is evident. This is the single greatest challenge to Christianity in Africa. People think they're worshipping their ancestral spirits when they are in fact worshipping familiar demonic spirits. The people of Africa see the supernatural power of the enemy. They believe in healings.

Richmond: From the book of Acts, we see that church planting is done most effectively through the demonstration of God's power. This gives us an effective witness. We know Africans believe in the supernatural. Church planters have to break through into their world to free them from the bondage. This can only be done by God. Church planting is not equivalent to starting a social club. Church planting is a supernatural act and must take place through supernatural means. God may heal somebody or bring deliverance to somebody. This is the evidence that the power of God has come among them.

In my training, I use Acts as the text on this whole issue to show that no church ever got planted unless the gospel was preached in the power of the Holy Spirit. In our preparation for this, we stress prayer—prayer as a means for opening doors, prayer as a means of equipping and preparing them for the context they are going into, prayer as a way of giving them spiritual understanding of the needs of the people.

We also pray for supernatural manifestations in the

name of Jesus. Church planters must have the attitude that this is going to happen. I don't want our church planters to be unprepared for the attacks of the enemy.

An American missionary and a local evangelist who did not have this kind of training went to preach in the Mount Darwin region in Zimbabwe. A demonized woman jumped at them in a demonic frenzy. The people, who had never heard the Word before, watched in dismay as the evangelist and the missionary took flight and ran for their lives. What kind of testimony is that to the people? They have seen the Christian message defeated.

In Africa, as elsewhere, the Church is not going to advance without supernatural encounters. Planting churches is an invasion of the enemy's kingdom. It's serious business. We must not shy away from this challenge.

Ted: As you have developed DAWN in an African soil, what problems have you encountered? What modifications have been necessary?

Richmond: As I read in the *DAWN 2000* book, the theory is to get denomination leaders to own the vision. They will then be able to mobilize their whole denominations around their own projects for multiplying congregations.

This does not tend to work well in Africa. Most often, church planting is not a popular ministry with denominational leaders. In Africa, people in high office don't get their hands dirty. But you can't be a church planter and expect to stay clean. Bible school and seminary-trained leaders will want to have an office job, do administrative work and enjoy their high position.

Many of our Bible schools help entrench this thinking. They reserve the upper levels of training for denominational leaders. Pastors, evangelists and church planters are given lowly training and are subsequently not respected. Many young men avoid going into church ministry for this reason. They seek out para-church work instead.

In the early Church, training happened in practice. You were equipped on the job. In the New Testament you found Christians everywhere preaching and planting new churches. We've got to get back to this more biblical way of doing things.

In the mean time, to target denominational leaders in the hope they will get down to the task of sharing and implementing church planting strategies is to actually miss the target in Africa. They are the ones that many times stand in the way of completing the Great Commission.

Ngwiza: It is important to understand the reality of tribalism and tribal regions within the countries of Africa. In many instances, these have defined and described the size of the world in which Africans exist. Consequently, regionalism is a strong factor in everything that happens.

A person's region is usually more important to him than the whole country. Certainly this is true in the political sense. People identify far more strongly with their home region, their tribal area. The more rural the people are, the more this is true.

It becomes very important for us to think along these lines as well. Looking back to the Target 2000 DAWN Congress in 1992, a lot of the national leaders were present, but many of the leaders closer to the grassroots did not come. One of the cries we received from these leaders was, "Come to our regions! Talk to us in our regions." If anything has given visibility to the DAWN vision and strategy it is that we have done exactly this. Now we must go back and help these leaders further as they develop regional DAWN strategies which—in the final analysis—add up to one great national strategy.

Richmond: The problems of language, geography and other issues that are much more pronounced in Africa are overcome when the vision takes root at the regional level. Pastors and workers at this level need encouragement. They need to know what is happening in other parts of the country. It is all too easy to feel bereft, as Elijah did— the "I-and-I-only-am-left" mentality. DAWN has played an important function in Zimbabwe by delivering God's message of encouragement: "You're not alone. There are thousands like you who have the same vision and commitment."

Freddie: DAWN can have a great impact right down to the most basic level in our society. We should be communicating DAWN to pastors, elders, church planters and denominational leaders throughout even the remotest regions of our nation.

Ted: The role of the missionary in Africa has changed greatly over the past few decades. How would you characterize the function and value of missionaries in Africa today?

Ngwiza: Attitude is everything. If missionaries come in as partners, as facilitators, as encouragers, they are most welcome. African pastors and leaders want to achieve more. They want to find what really works. The role of the missionary should be to help in this regard, to facilitate getting the job done more effectively.

By and large, the present day missionary has learned this, though you still get some examples of missionaries being heavy handed. Missionaries do want to be partners, to be ones who will pass on the vision and help where possible. We have accepted the involvement and vision which DAWN has represented in this light.

Richmond: Western missionaries are still viable in Africa. If God sends missionaries, they still have a job to do. When they no longer have a function, God will stop sending them. It is not up to national leaders to decide against missionaries.

Ted: What would you say has been the overall impact of DAWN?

Richmond: Leaders from different regions were drawn together by the DAWN vision in a way no other vision has ever succeeded. The magnet was the vision. We all had in our hearts a desire to see the nation discipled. God put this vision in our hearts. But DAWN fulfilled a critically important function by articulating and fleshing out the vision—and then pulling us all together behind the goals that this vision represents.

Ngwiza: We have encountered some resistance among mainline churches. Perhaps 40 percent of these leaders have heard of DAWN and understand the thinking. In terms of the evangelicals, the DAWN vision has impacted about 80 percent of the leaders in the evangelical churches. There is no doubt that DAWN has had a major impact in the process of making a disciple of our nation!

The spreading DAWN network

"As you might imagine, getting acquainted and working shoulder to shoulder with men like these has been one of the highlights of my life and ministry," says Olsen. These men, however, are not the only ones by far who have a zeal for discipling their own nation as well as the rest of the nations of Africa. There is now a growing network of leaders from several organizations who are banding together for this task.

Swaziland is a case in point. In their DAWN Congress held June 5-12, 1995, delegates embraced the vision to increase their number of church members from 168,200 to 480,000 by 2015. They would do this by doubling their number of churches from 3,256 to 6,500 in that 20-year period. They would also like to see the average size of local churches increase from 52 to 74 members.

The significance of this event, however, was not just the commitment that was made or the goals that were set. Rather, it was the network of organizations and leaders that came together that bodes well for future expansion.

For one thing, the OC International team that Olsen led for a while in Swaziland has fully embraced the DAWN vision. Under the leadership of Dean Carlson, they proved to be a strategic resource in the development of the DAWN project and Congress in Swaziland. OC in turn flew Ngwiza Mnkandla down from Zimbabwe to meet with top leaders from the three major branches of Christians. This was the first time they had ever come together with a united concern to disciple their nation. This show of unity is of historic proportions.

"This really got DAWN underway," Carlson told me. "Ngwiza shared what had happened through the DAWN project in Zimbabwe and gave a very direct prophetic challenge on cooperation in the discipling of their nation." The project was also reinforced when Xolisani Dlamini came from Zimbabwe to share his experiences of doing research for the DAWN project there.

"The ripple effect has not stopped at Swaziland," says Carlson. "After we presented our report at the Global Consultation on World Evangelization (GCOWE) in Korea in 1995, leaders from such neighboring countries as Botswana, Lesotho and others came and asked that Swazi Christians come and help get *their* DAWN projects started."

Nor does the network for filling all Africa with the presence of the incarnate Christ stop there. Ross Campbell of New Zealand, for example, continues to be a very key player. It was under his leadership that the DAWN-like project developed in Ghana in the 1980's. The particular genius of that project, which continues to this day, was their in-depth research. Campbell sent out a team of nine nationals to personally visit all 25,000 towns and villages with 50 or more population in the ten regions of the nation.

Among other startling data they discovered in their travels by car, motorbike, push bike, canoe and foot were 14,711 localities without a Protestant Church. This led to setting a goal of increasing the number of churches in the country from 22,000 in 1987 to 38,000 by 1996.

Along with Bob Waymire, Founder and President of Light International, Campbell was the one responsible for developing the profile of the AD2000 National Initiatives completely along the lines of DAWN. With his background and interest in Africa, he will be affirming the SCP vision all over the continent side-by-side with the rest of this growing network.

Working closely with him is Johan Combrinck, the AD2000 Coordinator for Africa. Combrinck is a passionate advocate of the DAWN strategy who served with Dawn Ministries for five years and is now one of our DAWN Associates. Through his own AFnet organization, Combrinck provides another vital link in the DAWN Africa network.

Along with his commitment to spreading the DAWN strategy, Combrinck has a particular concern for training national leaders for church planting and church multiplication. There are a number of training models to choose from in Africa, including the "portable school" movement that saw 10,000 churches planted in a three-year period in Zaire.[1]

My life for Africa

With the Zimbabwe model, we now have an example for the rest of Africa. Several of the key leaders have shared the vision in countries such as Ghana, Cote d'Ivoire, Zambia, Malawi, South Africa, Swaziland, Cameroon, Mozambique, Botswana, Namibia and elsewhere. More nations are being impacted all the time. Lessons are being learned and revisions constantly being made. DAWN, as it turns out, is not cast in iron. It has, instead, an inherent flexibility which accommodates contextual differences in the nations of Africa without compromising the vision.

"Now I'm giving my life to scour all 36 nations in Africa south of the Sahara for men like Ngwiza Mnkandla, Richmond Chiundiza and Freddie Gwanzura, men whose hearts already burn with a zeal for discipling their nations," Olsen told me in a phone conversation. "I know they are there. When such men are found and exposed to the DAWN vision, I know we will see a movement that will engulf all of black Africa in a mighty harvest. With the great responsiveness to the gospel in Africa and the proven DAWN model in Zimbabwe, I believe the strategy can sweep throughout the continent."

Speaking of sweeping the continent, this is already happening in the 55 nations south of the United States.

---

[1] Sheryl Wingerd, "Revolutionary 'portable schools' produce 10,000 churches in 3 years," *DAWN Report*, August, 1991. For more information, write Evangelism Resources, P.O. Box 8263, Lexington, KY 40533.

Chapter Six

Latin America: Key to World Evangelization

'This program integrates the evangelical strategies for the missionary takeover of the world and especially Latin America.'

Catholic Bishop in Venezuela

"I could not quite understand why evangelical congregations were multiplying all over until I read about the DAWN program."

In Dawn Ministries we somehow get used to hearing comments like this. *Lord, forgive us for taking you for granted.*

But this was a comment with a difference. It was written by Ovidio Perez Morales, Roman Catholic Bishop of the *Diocesis de Coro,* and it appeared in *"El Universal,"* a leading public newspaper in Caracas, Venezuela.

"This program integrates the evangelical strategies for the missionary takeover of the world and especially Latin America," he wrote. "It has been going on for years. And it is producing fruit."

The Bishop also had a keen understanding of the strategy and its implications.

"What is the purpose (of DAWN)?" he asked. "To occupy the land, a biblical expression. Its strategy? Fill every country with evangelical congregations: one for each small group of people in each existing ethnic or cultural environment. Its point of saturation? One church for every 500 to 1,000 persons in each homogeneous unit.... Work without rest; well planned, evaluated, concrete programs with their own distinct names; organization for growth in agile geometric proportion; permanent training; adequate financial support; and missionary activity without ceasing."

Lord, may what he writes truly become reality for your Church everywhere.

One final word from the Bishop in my mind characterizes what is actually happening in Latin America. "The evangelicals do not form a unit in the genuine sense," he concluded. "They are a constellation of churches and congregations. *But now they are uniting in DAWN, above and beyond differences, in order to occupy the world"* (emphasis mine).

The Bishop got it right

I believe the Lord first showed me the potential Latin America represented in 1976 when I became Director of Overseas Fields for Overseas Crusades, a position I held during the three years Luis Palau was president of the organization. Through no fault of Palau or OC, only minor gains in developing that potential were made during that time.

Twenty years later, however, I can see coming to pass that which the Lord placed on my mind and exactly what the good Bishop perceived was happening. God has been working in a mighty way in that region, perhaps for taking the key role in the completion of the Great Commission.

Just in terms of the DAWN strategy—on top of everything else the Lord is bringing to pass in Latin America—we see our ministry coming to a climax.

In a brief statement made before about 200 national

leaders gathered from 76 nations at the AD2000 and Beyond Movement "Thrust" meeting in December, 1995, for instance, I included a remark about Ecuador being the only one of 55 nations south of the United States that did not yet have a DAWN-type project underway. All other countries in the Caribbean, Central America and South America were in some stage of implementing a national strategy for filling every city, rural area and region with the presence of the incarnate Christ.

Later at that same conference, the loop was closed when a leader from Ecuador shouldered the responsibility for mobilizing the Church of that nation. As Berna Salcedo, Regional Coordinator for Dawn Ministries, expressed it, "*she* became our first *Juana* Knoxer." For it was Mary Aguilera, General Secretary for the Bible Society in Ecuador, who felt the hand of the Lord on her to commit herself to this task.

As is frequently the case, leaders of a national Bible Society have developed the kind of relationships with other national Church leaders that make it possible to bring them together for such a national mobilization.

In fact, it is always helpful and usually the case that some parachurch agency or mission gives this kind of support to a national DAWN-type project. OC International, Campus Crusade for Christ, Youth With A Mission, Operation Mobilization and others have played this role of providing needed infrastructure for a DAWN project. Literally scores of other denominations and organizations have cooperated in DAWN projects.

All this represents another beautiful expression of the Body of Christ coming together with a Kingdom mentality for the discipling of their nation.

Often, such organizations can move very quickly. Mary, for instance, that same week reported that the research had previously been done and that a tentative date for a DAWN Congress was already set for June of 1996!

An historic moment

Though it had always been in the back of my mind that Latin America had a vital role to play in world evangelization, it wasn't until I participated in the Second DAWN Congress sponsored by *Peru Para Cristo* October 31 to November 3, 1995, that everything now seemed in place for that to happen.

The congress itself was the best I had ever personally attended. That there was complete ownership of the vision by responsible leaders was powerfully evident. There was incredible unity and enthusiasm for the strategy displayed by the 1,182 registered delegates representing virtually every evangelical entity and every region of the nation. Almost every element of the congress program was right on target. The presentation of the data gathered by excellent Peruvian researchers clearly showed what had been accomplished and what needed still to be done in each city, state, rural area and jungle territory.

On a national level, they were able to report that the number of churches had jumped from about 10,000 that were in existence at the first DAWN Congress two years before to almost 14,000. Their detailed plans for extending the movement included 35 regional congresses to be held in 1996 in an effort to bring their number of churches to 19,000 by the end of 1997 and to their long-term goal of 50,000 churches by the year 2003.

"The highlight of the Congress," according to one observer, "came after Jim Montgomery spoke to the crowd about John Knox and his cry to the Lord, 'Give me Scotland or I die!' Rev. Jorge Romero came to the platform and asked the pastors if they would agree with John Knox and declare, 'Give me Peru or I die.' Every hand in the auditorium shot into the air as the call was issued a second, third and fourth time and as they shouted in unison, 'Give me Peru or I die.'"

That the Peru DAWN-type project was not an exceptional case for the region was evidenced by a smaller conference going on concurrently with the Peru for Christ Congress. This gathering consisted of 20 international leaders representing every region of nations south of the United States. They had come together to form a regional *Amanecer* (dawn) Committee for the purpose of seeing that the DAWN vision and strategy was being fully implemented in each of the 55 nations they represented.

Because of his brilliant leadership carried out with great humility, the group elected Dawn missionary Berna Salcedo, native of Colombia, as chairman of this ad hoc committee. Others solemnly accepted roles on the committee and responsibilities for a particular region.

Major immediate decisions were to gather a prayer summit for hundreds of gifted intercessors from all nations in 1996 and then to develop an International Congress for all Latin America in 1997. The latter would bring together many thousands of pastors and leaders for what would be the first DAWN-type congress for a whole region of the world.

Members of the new Amanecer Committee conservatively estimated that the combined goals for all the national projects in 55 countries would exceed 500,000 new churches by AD 2010. Added to the current 345,000, this would mean a total of 845,000 churches for a poplulation of 600 million or one church for every 710 people.

"The meeting flowed smoothly with much excitement as the men realized they were setting the course to bring every Latin American within reach of the gospel through saturating the regions with evangelical churches," reported Salcedo. "At the end, all were reminded that this was indeed an historic moment. God was beginning the process of uniting the Church of Jesus Christ in Latin America toward a common vision. The Amanecer document was read and signed by everyone committing themselves to see all of Latin America saturated with churches."

A *kairos* moment

It was my privilege to conclude this mini-conference. From the instant I was asked to do this weeks before, the Lord put on my heart what I was to share. I somehow knew then that it was a word from the Lord specifically for these dedicated men. My beloved and respected teammate, Berna Salcedo, captured the moment in the following written report:

> Then came a moment that all in attendance will not soon forget. Jim Montgomery stood to deliver a short Bible study and close the meeting in prayer. Instead, he gave a 20-minute speech which moved every person in the room.
>
> He told of his father who died of tuberculosis when he was just seven years old. His sister stated that everything Jim had accomplished in his ministry was because of the prayers of his father (during his five years in a TB sanitarium). The only document which remained from his father's extensive writings was an exposition of John 17.
>
> Jim shared how the Lord had used John 17:1 to lead him to begin Dawn Ministries and how he was now using John 17:4 to tell him that he had completed one phase of his ministry. The Amanecer (DAWN) vision had been caught by the leaders in the room and Jim was to pass the baton to them to finish the work.
>
> Everyone was silent. Alberto De Luca from Argentina spoke for the group and expressed his awe and amazement that Jim would pass his vision on to the others and commission them to go forth and complete the task. He stated that this was an awesome responsibility and a real challenge.
>
> What a moment! Everyone left with a new sense of calling and commitment to the vision for the whole world.

It was, of course, a very special moment for me as well.

For one thing, I can think of only a few occasions in my life when my speaking had such a profound impact. For another, it really did mark a significant milestone in my allotted 70 years or so. The strategy had been developed and was proliferating around the world. The organization God had raised up to spread the vision was flourishing. By now I had turned all administrative and fund-raising responsibilities of the mission to Steve Steele, our newly appointed CEO. The ministry of sharing the vision and equipping national leaders around the world had long since been in the hands of our regional coordinators. These consisted of Ted Olsen for Africa, Wolfgang Fernández for East and West Europe plus the Arab world, Jack Dennison for North America, Roy Wingerd for South Asia, Steve Spaulding for East Asia and Berna Salcedo for Latin America. Our most recent addition was Mike Steele who was serving in several needed capacities.

Just for the record, however, I was not going into retirement. I am still working full time and still have ultimate responsibility for the mission as I continue to serve as president. What I said to these men was that from now on I would be telling the world just what God was doing through them as they carried out the vision. In other words, my continuing ministry until my fingers wore out and my mind turned to mush would primarily be to carry out the intent of my life's verse: "Write the vision; make it plain upon tablets, so he may run who reads it" (Hab. 2:2). This book is one evidence of that continuing ministry.

The moment also crystallized in my mind the significance of what was happening in Latin America for the whole world. The bits and pieces of events and activities here and there over a number of years suddenly formed a complete picture. God was using the forces of history, culture, geography, economy, the Roman Catholic Church, a vibrant and exploding evangelical movement and now the great openness to the gospel throughout the region to prepare a mighty force for a significant role in completing the task of world evangelization. It dawned on me that we were in a *kairos* moment with potentially eschatological significance. A force had been prepared and was being prepared for the completion of the Great Commission and the end of the age.

These are heady words, I know, but walk with me through some of the logic of these statements.

Experienced, committed leadership

First of all is the caliber and commitment of the leaders involved. Those men who formed the regional association for the discipling of all the nations of Latin America and promoting a pioneer missionary movement are exceptional. They are not always the ones who are household names in international Church circles, as significant and important as such leaders are. Rather, they are the ones with a proven ministry at the national level. They have been through the process of mobilizing the Church in their individual countries and are now taking active leadership on a regional basis.

Adonai Leiva of El Salvador, for example, is a very conservative, very balanced Christian leader. And committed! He has seen some of his 50-member Campus Crusade staff die in taking the *Jesus* film into the very areas of El Salvador occupied by guerrillas—even into their headquarters! With his ministry to many denominations, people think of him as the Apostle for El Salvador.

On top of his heavy duties in running the Crusade program, Leiva has been the prime mover for the DAWN-type project for about nine years. Since the first Congress in 1987, he has so mobilized the Church as to see their number of congregations increase from about 3,000 to 6,000 as of their second Congress in 1993. This represents a very high AAGR of 12 percent.

Their goal is an additional 2,000 churches and one for every 500 people by the end of 1996, the centennial of evangelical missions in El Salvador.

His role on the Amanecer Committee is to shepherd all the DAWN projects in the seven nations of Central America.

Israel Brito, on the other hand, is determined to see strong DAWN projects flourishing throughout the Caribbean. Motivated by research that indicated denominations were in decline, Brito is the one who mortgaged his home to raise the initial $25,000 for the Congress in the Dominican Republic. The Congress delegates representing virtually every church in the nation not only saw the debt repaid but committed themselves to the goal of 12,000 churches by AD 2002.

The 3,000 churches reported at the first DAWN Congress in 1992 increased to more than 5,000 by the second Congress in 1994, an incredible AAGR of 29 percent! In addition to serving the DAWN movement in his own land and throughout the Caribbean, Brito is also head of Conecar, the evangelical alliance for the Caribbean.

Tomás Moreno was not only an active pastor but head of his denomination when he caught the DAWN vision at a meeting in Florida. Since then he has mobilized the Church in Venezuela and has been active in communicating the vision and helping national committees in several other Latin nations.

As for Venezuela, careful research before their first Congress in 1992 had revealed 6,000 churches in the country. In the next two years an additional 4,000 churches were started. Growth in those two years was so fast that they increased their original target from 20,000 churches to 22,000 by AD 2002.

Alberto De Luca of Argentina was pleased with the revival fires that were burning in his native land. Then Berna Salcedo shared with him and a group of other leaders growth statistics for the national Churches of Latin America. Amazed that Argentina had one of the lowest growth rates for church planting in the whole region, De Luca went right to work. He called a meeting of about 100 leading pastors and presented the DAWN vision.

From this meeting emerged a national committee that planned a DAWN congress for late in 1996. De Luca has also taken responsibility for keeping the DAWN movement alive and prospering in the whole southern cone.

I wish it were practical to give brief biographical sketches like this of every Amanecer Committee member, to tell the story of Eliseo Escobar and the plan for another 50,000 churches in Mexico, of the problems and frustrations faced by Josué Reyes in developing DAWN in Colombia and of many more. These are committed men who are standing in the gap for their nations and their regions (Ez. 22:30). Without any organizational ties to Dawn Ministries, without any financial support from North America, these "John Knoxers" are truly living out the cry to "Give me my country or I die."

"What is happening in Latin America," Salcedo said after the Peru meetings, "is that we now have the whole continent ready for harvest and the key leaders in place to see the harvest is gathered.

"Our leaders left this organizational and planning meeting of the Amanecer Committee saying, 'This is the most important meeting I have ever been to in my whole life.' They were saying they felt the Lord had put them in the position of guiding the Church of the whole continent. There had been many movements and events in Latin America, but the Lord had brought the right people together with the right agenda and strategy to make an impact on the continent and the world. God is moving, awakening the Latin Church for world evangelization."

A passion for the unreached

While the Peru for Christ Congress was in session, I was asked to meet with some of the foreign and national leaders of the Christian and Missionary Alliance denomination. It was in their largest church in Lima that the Congress was being held. *I* wanted to talk about the DAWN strategy. *They* wanted to talk about sending Latin missionaries overseas. This, for me, opened the whole topic of the role of Latin Americans in completing the frontier missionary task of beginning church-planting movements among the unreached peoples of the world.

By its very nature, such cross-cultural ministry is never easy. It always involves moving from a culture with one set of values and frame of reference to another. Everything that seemed natural, obvious and right back home no longer "works." Still, it is always easier for some individuals—those blessed with the missionary gift—and even for some whole nationalities or regions of peoples to bridge the gap than others.

The Latin American vision for the unreached is actually at three levels. First is for the tribal groups and other hidden elements of society in their individual countries. Second is for the Latin American "door." This is the huge Amazon basin largely in Brazil but including parts of seven other nations in the Northwest corner of the continent. The vision of the Amanecer Committee for this vast territory that contains most of the unreached peoples of Latin America is 100,000 new churches by AD 2010.

Then there is their zeal for the "uttermost parts" of the world represented primarily by the nations of the 10/40 window, that geographical section of the world that runs from 10 to 40 degrees North and from the western rim of Africa to the eastern tip of Indonesia. It is in this "window" that a great majority of the peoples live that are still without a viable Christian movement in their midst. (More on this in the next chapter.)

Mike Steele, our newest Dawn Ministries missionary, saw how God had prepared Latin Americans for pioneer ministry in a flash of insight at the Peru for Christ Congress. He was video taping a procession of flags of the nations during the Congress opening ceremony when one of the girls holding a flag from an Islamic nation passed by. She wore Arab dress and had a shawl wrapped around her face.

"You would swear when you looked at this girl that she was an Arab," he says. "When I took her picture the Lord said to me, 'You see how easy it is going to be for them to penetrate the "window"? She is Peruvian, but dressed like that, she almost looks middle eastern. She is perfectly adapted physically to be accepted within that culture.' I said, 'Praise you, Jesus!'"

Steele, who comes from several years of international contacts in the high-tech business world, connected this experience with other fresh insights in his first months as a missionary. "When I look back two years ago to my first experience with a group of leaders from all over the world," he said to some of us at Dawn Ministries, "it stands out most in my mind how closed, how divided so many cultures are.

"But when you go to Latin America, you find they're friendly. They're open. God has uniquely molded their culture and personality to be most naturally suited to take the gospel everywhere. No other group in the world is so open, so free to express its joy in Christ. They have a genuine care for the peoples that I have not witnessed in other cultures. They want to go to the whole world, they want to understand the cultures, they want to be part of seeing the gospel spread everywhere."

Berna Salcedo, himself a Latin from Colombia, mentioned many other specifics. "Other cultures and peoples have permeated our societies," he said. "Slaves from Africa have influenced our culture. We have been colonized by Europeans. Look at Peru. They have a Japanese president! The Middle East has impacted us. We call these people 'Turkos,' though they are not only from Turkey. We have all kinds of paganism and demonic activity such as the spiritism in Brazil. We have Hinduism in Surinam. Latinos are aware of all these forces and have assimilated them. Latin Christians won't be shocked by anything they see in the 10/40 window countries.

"Then you look at the political and economic world. We have never colonized anybody nor made enemies in world wars. Economically, we are struggling in poverty like everybody else. We are a threat to no one. We are in the same boat as the rest of the third world.

"The great thing is that our people are praying for the unreached peoples of the world. And they are ready to go. The COMIBAM missionary conference for all Latin America has played a tremendous role in missions awareness. I think many evangelicals of Latin America are ready to pay whatever price is necessary."

And a strategy as well!

Another factor that works to the advantage of Latin Christians is simply their vision, experience and zeal for church multiplication. One of the concerns I have had for the two-thirds missionary movement, a movement that soon will have more missionaries on the field than the West, is the major emphasis on the number being sent and very little on what they will do when they get there. Studies indicate that the average stay of two-thirds world missionaries on the field has been very short. In many cases they have not been adequately trained either for cross-cultural work or on how to make a strategic impact. Discouragement quickly sets in.

"What Latin missionaries will bring to pioneer missions," says Salcedo, "is the best method to reach a whole nation, whether reached or unreached. That is saturation church planting. The Amanecer Committee is in a position to impact the whole missionary enterprise of Latin America with that vision and training.

"Who knows best how to communicate the vision for discipling a whole nation? Those who have been involved in a DAWN strategy at home. That's why the DAWN movement in Latin America will be the key. My point is that not only is God using us to bring all Latin America to be saturated with that vision, but also that we go from Latin America to the whole world with the same vision. It will be a major cross-cultural work, with a major hurdle being the learning the languages, but it will be the same vision. Working alongside the established churches in the 10/40 window, Latins can play a major role in evangelization and church planting.

"The sheer volume is incredible. We're not talking about the Church in one country determining to do a work. We're talking about a continent, a whole region of the world and the power behind that, determining to make disciples of the unreached nations of the world."

Tried by fire

The moral fiber of Latin Christians is an added, less tangible, ingredient. "The Church has learned endurance through the hardships they have faced," says Jorge Osorio, one of the Peruvian leaders who is also on the regional Amanecer Committee. "This has produced a very special breed of church planters for Latin America and the rest of the world."

He related the story told to him by a friend as an example. Members of the notorious Shining Path movement came to his friend's church. After the leaders of the congregation were herded into a small room, a grenade was thrown into their midst. Miraculously, they came out unharmed and brushing off debris from the explosion. "We would rather go into the lion's den with the Lord than deny our faith," they said.

The miracle God performed in the life of a man we can identify only as "Jaime" is another incredible example of what some Latins have experienced.

Two days after the Colombian army arrested Rodrigo Orejuela, the number one most wanted person in the world and leader of the Cali cartel, Berna Salcedo flew to Armenia, Colombia, where the government planned to carry out their vengeance. He was invited by Josué Reyes, John Knoxer for the "Colombia Today and Tomorrow" DAWN project. He needed assistance in training 25 carefully selected workers in the DAWN research process. That is when Salcedo met Jaime, one of the former cartel leaders.

"I learned that Jaime had worked for a drug cartel for several years," Salcedo reported. "In the process, he amassed a huge personal fortune. During a war between the cartels, Jaime's life was always in jeopardy. He moved constantly, always sleeping with a gun in his hand.

"Ultimately, all his precautions couldn't save him. A gunman hiding behind the building where he was staying one night shot him several times from a distance of about six feet. After an ensuing scuffle, Jaime began to examine his body. He should have been dead, but to his surprise none of the bullets had penetrated his body!

"'I couldn't believe it!' says Jaime. 'I touched my body time after time to be sure I was still in this world. It had to be a miracle!'

"That same night, Jaime knelt before the Lord and asked forgiveness and for a change in his life. What he didn't know was that many miles away, his mother was praying that same prayer. That night, for the first time in his turbulent, crazy, life, Jaime slept with a Bible in his hand instead of a gun!

"Jaime joined a local church where he hid for almost a year. But he was not happy. He needed to share the gospel with his 'friends' before his conversion, especially the *capos* (drug lords). Risking his life, he jumped over all obstacles and zigzagged past many dangers to reach their hideout. Once safely there, he shared the gospel with them. Since then we have learned from official sources that many drug traffickers have turned their lives over to Jesus.

"As for Jaime, he could have ended up dead or like six key people of the Cali cartel who have either been arrested or have surrendered to the authorities. Instead, he has become one of the leaders of the DAWN project in 'coffee land,' the region of Colombia where the best coffee in the world is grown."

With his new life in Christ and zeal for his own nation, Jaime now says, "I am convinced that the DAWN vision of saturation church planting is the answer to take the gospel to every corner of our nation so that many people, some like me, can be touched by Christ!"

'Return to your country or die'

Converts like Jaime had already known danger, deprivation and daring before coming to know the Lord. Like Lok Mani Bhandiri of Nepal (see Chapter Ten), their pre-Christian background makes them excellent leaders for the eternal task of discipling a nation. But young men and women brought up in Christian homes have an ability to cope as well.

Jesuel, for example, was a single young man sent to Peru by his church in Brazil. A week later he was discussing with a group of workers as to when, where and how they might plant a new church. In the midst of the session a demon calling himself the "Prince of Peru" appeared to him. "Return to your own country if you do not want to die in Peru," he said.

He rebuked the demon, but in one week became so ill that doctors gave up hope for his recovery. As he lay struggling for his life, a pastor in the city was praying. The Lord impressed on him to go to the hospital to pray for this unknown young man. He did, and Jesuel was healed.

Soon after, Jesuel went to a city in the North where no church existed. After four weeks of evangelizing, no one had been converted. Nevertheless, he persisted in prayer. One day as he walked past a Roman Catholic church, he noticed that it was closed and learned that no priest had been there for six months. He developed a friendship with the caretaker and led him to the Lord.

"Why don't we call the people for a mass," the caretaker suggested one day. They rang the bell and people streamed in from everywhere. More than 100 were converted. Jesuel and his friend continued to gather the converts and inquirers for further meetings.

When priests in nearby towns heard what was happening, they spread rumors that Jesuel was there only to seduce the women. Jesuel fled for his life, but refused to cave in. He planted churches in five other towns before returning to Brazil.

Recovered from his ordeal and married, he now says, "My wife and I have decided to go back to Peru to plant more churches."

Perhaps the Church of Latin America has not suffered deprivation and persecution as much as the Church of some nations. Still, the endurance they have learned is another significant factor added to the others that has prepared them for their role in world evangelization.

The "Mission 10/40" plan

"There is such a zeal for pioneer mission work among Latins," says Salcedo, "that I could go anywhere and ask 'How many of you want to go to the 10/40 window?' Time and again we would have 10,000 raise their hands."

Salcedo and the Amanecer Committee have a much more in-depth plan than that, however. Among other things, they want to avoid what they perceive to be the mistakes of evangelicals who poured into the nations of the former Soviet Union with huge amounts of money but with little understanding or long-range strategy.

The vision of the plan they call "Mission 10/40" is very

simple in concept. It is to see a missionary movement develop in Latin America that is thoroughly committed to the SCP concept and thoroughly trained for cross-cultural ministry. A mid-term goal would be to see 2,000 such missionaries deployed beginning at the end of the decade. Each missionary would be expected to see 100 or more churches planted by themselves, their converts and their trainees. If accomplished, such a plan would produce 200,000 churches over a period of time. Through the impact and influence of these first 2,000 missionaries, the vision is to see another 20 to 25 thousand follow in their steps.

As of the end of 1995, the first 100 potential missionaries from Latin America had already been identified. These were to be sent to England to receive training by experienced DAWN leaders there before heading for a targeted 10/40 nation. Once there, they would learn the language, receive further training by teams of missionaries already in place and then be sent out to establish the first church in each of about 75 regions of that land.

This first group of 100 would soon be followed by the second 100 and then the third and fourth until 2,000 missionaries from the nations of Latin America are on location among unreached peoples.

"The way I'm sharing this in Latin America," says Salcedo, "is that this is our tithe, our offering to the Lord. God has greatly blessed us, now we have to bless others."

Salcedo feels there will be little problem in recruiting, training and sending at least 200 such missionaries from each Latin nation. "There are already many who have committed their lives to this endeavor," he says. "In my country, Colombia, there are already about 250 being trained in just the North coast region. This is a preparation and training time. It is an in-depth, long-range process.

"We want to do this right so that in time we will not only have a solid ministry but that we will be a model for

Africa and Asia as well. But right now, Latin America is the key. This is where the missionaries are. There is no other continent with our potential right now.

"What the Lord showed Mike about the girl in Peru was prophetic. I haven't observed that other leaders have seen this yet, but right now Latin America is a key to the unreached peoples of the world."

A continent at prayer

Behind the leadership, the vision, the strategy, the commitment, the plan and a people prepared by the Lord for a significant role in world evangelization is a continent at prayer.

Berna Salcedo saw this firsthand through an experience in the little nation of Dominica when he flew there in the summer of 1991. He had been invited by Peter Augustine, President of the Evangelical Alliance of Dominica, to share the DAWN strategy with church leaders.

Handing his passport to an airport official, he noticed his face turn red. He soon found himself being submitted to interrogation by the Central Intelligence Agency of Dominica. This lasted three hours, after which he was thrown in jail.

The week before, Dominican police had arrested 12 Colombians for transporting drugs and had since been receiving threats to blow up the island. At the sight of his Colombian passport, Salcedo was immediately suspect.

While he was with the police, pastors and members from several churches of different denominations were waiting for him at a local church. When they heard he had been arrested, they began to pray intensively.

He was set free that same night and arrived at the church at 11:30 p.m. where people were still waiting. They praised God, some of them with tears, for his answer to their prayers. They also realized that strong spiritual warfare had begun.

The next day, 60 key denominational leaders decided to implement the DAWN strategy in Dominica and to organize prayer cells in each village of the island. A tremendous prayer revival had begun. Within a few weeks, 25 permanent prayer groups were praying for the nation and for the DAWN strategy. Sixty prayer warriors spent a night going around the island in a boat, praying for each city and village as they passed by.

Discovering later that Satanic sects were visiting evangelical churches at midnight to curse them, 150 intercessors separated the whole month of November to fast and pray.

If it was raining in the Caribbean, it was pouring in the rest of the region.

In August of 1991, for example, 250 pastors and intercessors met in a gathering called "Cry for Peru." These men went to this seminar on prayer and fasting and a great revival started! The participants committed to raise an army of 10,000 intercessors to pray that Peru be saturated with Christ-centered evangelical churches. During the 1995 Congress, 200 of these intercessors were on site and in constant prayer. Surely this is part of the backdrop of what is now happening in that nation.

Another 10,000 people in a single church in Colombia made the decision to pray 15 minutes daily for their nation and the DAWN strategy, called "Colombia Today and Tomorrow." Among these people, 300 committed themselves to fast for a time every week. After many years of frustration, Colombia now has a vibrant project aiming at 50,000 new churches.

A church in Maracaibo, Venezuela, started a two-hour prayer service for their nation every Monday. It's the most attended service of the week. In Costa Rica a tremendous revival began among teenagers with more than 1,000 youths meeting regularly to fast and pray for the nation. In Guatemala, a church pastored by Harold Caballeros sent people out two by two to pray for every town and city of the country.

Since 1991 when the above, selected, activities were first reported, the prayer movement has continued to explode. This has led the Amanecer Committee to believe the time is ripe for the 1996 prayer summit. Bringing unity and focus to the prayer movements all over the region in this way will provide further spiritual foundation for their role in world evangelization.

It is Salcedo's vision that by God's grace an army of one million intercessors throughout all of Latin America and the Caribbean will be raised up to pray for the five hundred thousand churches that are needed to disciple the region by the year 2000 and for Latin America's outreach to the peoples of the 10/40 window, a region where DAWN, against all odds, is beginning to make a significant impact.

Chapter Seven

India: DAWN and the Unreached

'All the ends of the earth will remember and turn to the Lord, and all the families of the nations will bow down before him...'

Psalm 22:27

Latin America with its centuries of at least a form of Christianity, a current responsiveness to the gospel and a vibrant evangelical Church is one thing.

At the opposite end of the spectrum are the people groups of the world that have yet to see even the beginnings of a church-planting movement among them. Almost by definition, it would be easy to conclude that DAWN is not designed for and would not work in such nations.

For how is it possible to "mobilize the whole Body of Christ in a whole nation to fill that nation with evangelical congregations" if there is no viable Body of Christ there to begin with?

Still, in Dawn Ministries we persist in the belief that the Lord would have us work towards the goal of seeing a DAWN strategy underway in *every* nation of the world by AD 2000. Also by definition, this implies DAWN covering every people group in the world whether currently "reached" or "unreached." The nation of India provides a good case study relating to DAWN and the unreached.

One Million Churches for India

Actually, it wasn't until the early 1980's that we began looking at the possibility of a DAWN project that would cover a significant portion of the unreached peoples of the world. That is when the Lord began opening the India door for us. Here was a vast nation with roughly 15 percent of the world's population and 30 percent of its unreached peoples in somewhere between 3,500 and 4,600 (depending on your definition) separate people groups.

There was no doubt in our minds that a DAWN project for India represented a degree of difficulty far greater than any other project to that date. In time, we became aware of the fact that there was a strong Church in the southern part of India, that a miserly .15 percent of the people across the Hindi belt in the Northern part of the country with its population of 700,000,000 were believers, that many of the states in India were bigger than most countries of Europe, that India had the second largest Muslim population of the world, that even for Indian national missionaries the task required crossing formidable cultural barriers, and that there were many other hard facts about this overwhelming mosaic of "nations" precariously held together in the country called "India."

But we believed God had raised up the DAWN vision and strategy to embrace the whole of the Great Commission, the discipling of *all* nations and people groups. We had begun by accepting invitations from those nations where there was a Church of some strength and good responsiveness to the gospel. Now it was time to launch out into the deep.

Initial meeting in Madras

At the time, I was editing the *Global Church Growth* Magazine with Donald McGavran whose church growth movement emerged from his long years in India. With these connections, I began hearing about Indian mission agencies that had set goals and were implementing plans for church multiplication. When my list of such projects reached about 25, I realized perhaps something of significance was going on. Was this evidence that God was preparing the way for a church multiplication project of national proportions?

I wrote to Bobby Gupta of the Hindustan Bible Institute (HBI) suggesting we bring together leaders of these ministries and any others he was familiar with to see if they might be the catalyst for a national DAWN-type project.

I had only recently met Gupta, but had learned a bit of his background. His father had founded HBI and a host of interconnected ministries with the passion of reaching all India for Christ. This mantle would fall on his son Paul Robert "Bobby" Gupta. Though he was young and in many ways untested in the arena of national leadership, he took my suggestion and called for a Consultation On National Strategy (CONS) in 1987. (The initials were kept, but the name was later changed to "Council on National Service," a sponsoring body for what has become the DAWN India project.)

It was my privilege to share the DAWN concept with this relatively small group of 57 evangelical leaders in a setting that we in Dawn Ministries refer to as the "Initial Meeting." It is in such gatherings that the DAWN vision is first presented to a representative group of leaders. If the vision is not caught at this time, we usually conclude that the nation is not ready for a DAWN strategy.

That this was the right group became evident when I asked them to picture India with a church for every 1,000 people. They caught this vision and began dreaming and planning for one church in every one of 600,000 villages and 400,000 colonies (city neighborhoods): a total of one million churches for India! As noted, this would require a massive thrust into the unreached peoples of the nation.

The national committee formed at this gathering asked

Vararuchi Dalavai to serve as Director of this fledgling movement. Dalavai, Asia Coordinator for Bible Centered Ministries and AD2000 Coordinator for South Asia, spent the next seven years sharing this vision through a host of seminars, consultations, appointments and various publications. Some research was also begun. At the same time, a plan was being implemented for a national congress for August, 1990, in the central city of Hyderabad.

To soft pedal any possible adverse secular publicity about a movement designed to Christianize—to disciple—the primarily Hindu nation of India, the congress with about 750 official delegates convened under the banner of "The First All-India Congress on Church Development." In a further effort to contextualize the DAWN process, it was felt important to invite high visibility speakers whether or not they had personally embraced the DAWN vision. That and the lack of any in-depth research and the setting of specific denominational and mission goals kept this from being a classic DAWN congress.

Nonetheless, the dream of one million churches for India was mentioned so many times that perhaps by sheer force of repetition the idea caught on.

500,000 more churches by AD

Here's how it impressed at least one lady! In the years prior to the congress, she had ministered with her husband in a tribal group. She tried to carry on the ministry after his death in 1985, but found it difficult. She came to the congress ready to give up, but the Lord met her there.

"As I sat in the meeting," she later testified, "I was telling the Lord that I would like to plant 20 churches by the turn of the century." That didn't seem like enough, so she asked the Lord to help her plant 50. By the time of the second congress in 1995, she had started 65 and still had five more years to go!

Happily, she was not the only one bitten by the DAWN

bug in 1990. For the fact that there *was* a second congress in 1995 is indication in itself that the DAWN idea had not gone the way of all flesh after an original burst of enthusiasm. Actually, with CONS now under the leadership of Bobby Gupta, the Second Congress looked more like DAWN than ever before.

Concerning goal setting, for example, each of the 1,000 or so delegates was expected to send in his or her written goals ahead of time. A total of 610 of the delegates representing a great majority of the churches and missions in the nation actually did. These ranged from local churches that had decided to plant one daughter congregation to missions and denominations that reported goals of anywhere from 100 to 1,000 new churches. One ministry set a goal of 5,000 and two major projects were expecting to plant 100,000 and 300,000 churches respectively by AD 2000!

All together, these goals added up to 491,216 new churches projected for the year 2000. Since not quite all evangelicals were represented at the congress, it didn't seem unreasonable to round this off to a specific goal for the nation of 500,000 new churches by the end of the decade.

Though the ultimate target of one million total churches was not set aside, this goal of half a million additional churches by the year 2000 was generally accepted. With an estimated 200,000 churches already in existence, that would bring the nation up to 700,000 by AD 2000 and leave 300,000 churches to go in the next decade or so.

But can the goals be reached?

To casually throw around numbers of this magnitude might seem a bit capricious, especially when it is understood that the majority of these churches need to be planted under most difficult cross-cultural circumstances among unreached people groups. It is much easier, of course, to set goals than to reach them. Still, the individual stories as well as the massive projects speak of an increasing army ready for any sacrifice to accomplish the task.

A letter I received a few months ago graphically describes the commitment of more and more thousands of workers coming to the fore.

"Greetings to you in the precious name of our Lord and Savior Jesus Christ," it began in typical third-world grace and devotion. "Yesterday it was Shivarathri (a Hindu Festival). My evangelist and area coordinator along with two trainees were gathered with about 20 people who had asked to be baptized.

"Suddenly a crowd of more than 50 people attacked the coordinator and me. They took our Bible, diary, reports and about 400 rupees plus my nice new shirt. They burned all these in front of the people.

"They also beat us badly with sticks, helmets and stones. Blood poured from the nose and mouth of the coordinator and both of us were covered with blood. Two of my teeth are loosened and they hit our stomachs.

"With that kind of pain I am writing this letter. The police took us to the hospital, but we are unable to walk. One trainee was also badly beaten and we are still searching for him. We praise God that we can have an experience like Paul and Silas in Philippi. We know the Lord is going to do great miracles in the future in this hard state."

Ready to die

Many of the church planters Bobby Gupta himself is training at the Hindustan Bible Institute have had similar experiences. Though HBI is located in the more Christianized area of Madras, the church planters are sent out to the "hard states." As of this writing, more than 1,600 have graduated from this specific program, one of many ministry streams offered at the school. These graduates have started 247 new congregations towards their goal of 1,000 churches among unreached peoples by AD 2000.

"These men," says Gupta, "are literally ready to die to spread the gospel of Jesus Christ in India."

To back up his statement, he reports that when one group of 57 of his church planters were asked how many of them had been beaten during their year of training, about 20 of them raised their hands! One of them gave this testimony:

"Two years after my graduation as a church planter," he said, "religious militants came into my village. After destroying my home, they went to the church I had planted and killed the two new believers they found there. Then they set fire to the church.

"I stood in the nearby river watching my church burn. Do you know why I was in the river? Because *in the light of the burning church I was baptizing 11 more converts!"*

Anecdotes like this tend to pop up everywhere in India. While they don't add up to one million churches, they do make the goals sound more believable.

Ratsasam, for instance, was a Hindu lady living in a small village. She was separated from her alcoholic husband who still tortured her for not bearing any children after four years of marriage. Her life was further devastated when she developed tuberculosis.

Then pastor Raja Clarence Maruthaiah, himself a converted Hindu priest, arrived in the village. After hearing pastor Clarence preach in a nearby home, Ratsasam trusted the Lord, was instantly healed of her tuberculosis and a year later gave birth to a baby girl.

Villagers were so impressed that 42 Hindus turned to Christ and formed just one of 477 new Assemblies of God churches planted that year.

Reaching Hindus *with* Hindus!

One almost bizarre plan for multiplying congregations in the Hindi belt of North India was developed by a man we will call Dr. J. D. Kamar. His full story was told to Sheryl

Wingerd and reported in our *DAWN Report* Magazine (May 1995). It was thought best not to use his real name, but the story is true.

Dr. J. D. Kamar, a surgeon, spent 18 years serving the people in about 100 villages of Madhya Pradesh. He helped establish a hospital, he provided seeds for villagers to develop gardens and he built lakes which he stocked with African fish. As a result, the health, nutritional level and economy of the people greatly improved.

But he also wanted to see converts gathered into local churches.

He asked his denominational leaders for young people that could be trained. They declined. He asked parents in his local church to send their kids. Again the answer was "no." He finally asked the kids themselves but they said, "We'd rather get good jobs as engineers and doctors."

He returned to his villages somewhat discouraged but not defeated. Looking around, the startling thought occurred to him that perhaps Hindu villagers themselves could be trained to plant churches. "Who would be better than the people who live here?" he thought.

Not long after, some Hindu tribal boys came looking for jobs. "O.K., I'll give you jobs," he said, "but it's a different kind of job." He explained that they would be planting Christian churches. They were interested!

Kamar got permission from the boys' parents to send them to his training school in North India, even after the warning that both the boys and their fathers might become Christians!

Five months later, ten boys returned, now as eager new believers in Christ. Looking at a map, they each chose five villages and were sent out two by two. They were paid a small salary and were expected to work ten hours a day. After no more than three years, the subsidy would be withdrawn and the young pastors would be supported by their new congregations.

The boys, called "village-level workers" by Dr. Kamar, spent their weekdays discerning and binding the spirits over each village. On Saturday nights they held worship meetings where they shared the gospel, healed the sick and cast out demons. Services often lasted till 2:00 a.m. Many came to know Christ in those meetings. Their special targets were the influential leaders of the villages.

Saturday mornings were spent at Dr. Kamar's house for worship, prayer, fasting and discipleship training. The result was that they became a tremendous, close-knit team that planted 42 house churches or prayer cells ranging from 4 to 15 members in the 50 villages in five months.

In the meantime another batch of ten had come back from Bible school ready to go out to fifty more villages. Dr. Kamar is planning to add 10 workers every five months.

If this were the end of the story, it would still be a good one. But Dr. Kamar sees this approach in light of reaching all India for Christ. He notes that the states of India are divided into districts which contain from 2,000 to 4,000 villages. Each district is then divided into 10 blocks with 200 to 400 villages.

His plan is to see that once village workers are experienced in one block they will take another block within that district or move on to be district leaders over about 100 church planters. His goal is to see a church planted in every one of the 3,000 to 4,000 villages of his district.

Dr. Kamar hopes to see his model adopted by others in Madhya Pradesh and is now looking for key leaders who will adopt each district, come to his farm for training and spread the movement throughout the state.

The strategy appears to be indefinitely reproducible. The only cost is a small salary for the church planter for a period of three years. This cost is covered through the profits of a farm Kamar operates. Furthermore, there seems to be a large supply of young Hindus that want a church-planting "job."

These workers are effectively trained in the Word, in spiritual warfare and in planting churches. They know their own culture well and are accustomed to living on the village economy. Best of all, church planting is the result of evangelism and conversion from among Hindus in northern India, not growth through transfers or reaching nominal Christians.

The circle or boundary for this "outside-in" strategy is one district of one state of one nation. Working back from that, Kamar envisions saturating that district with one church in every one of the villages of the district. It seems to be one viable model for helping to reach the overall goal of 500,000 new churches in India by the end of this decade.

Discipling a whole state

Another saturation church planting project that actually covers a whole state in like manner grew out of the ministry of evangelist Sadhu Chellapa. I was able to get his story in an interview during the 1995 Congress.

Though he was living in Madras, the city where CONS was headquartered, he had not heard of DAWN until well into 1993. Maybe it was because he was so immersed in the growth of his own ministry. Starting with a mini-congregation of seven people in 1973, he had seen it grow to 7,400 members plus 75 daughter churches by 1995!

That's an Average Annual Growth Rate of 37 percent just in the mother church! Up to 60 percent of these new members were converts from Hinduism and a tiny percent from among Muslims.

When he was introduced to the DAWN concept, as you can well imagine, he was ready for it. This expanded his own vision to increase his number of daughter congregations to 1,000 by AD 2000 and see his total membership grow to 20,000. He is also taking active leadership in the Madras city project with its vision of increasing from 1,400 to 8,000 churches and in the state-wide project with its need of 50,000 churches by the end of the decade.

This emerging state-wide project is actually more like the classic DAWN project in such places as England. The states of India are so huge and the differences between them so great that they resemble separate nations. In fact, it is through such state-wide projects that CONS is now implementing DAWN throughout the rest of the country. Several states have already held DAWN congresses and more are being planned for covering the whole country.

DAWN from the bottom up

Still another almost unbelievable national project that actually pre-dates DAWN in India is called "Mission 21 India." The approach of this strategy was to divide India into 850 Million People Units or "MPU's." The goal was to plant 1,000 churches in each MPU within ten years for a total of 850,000.

The plan calls for training and deploying 20 church planters in each of the 850 regions of one million population. The goal for each missionary is to start 50 Witnessing Prayer Cells or what might be called "cell" or "house churches" in a ten-year period. This would produce 1,000 congregations in each area of one million people or a total of 850,000 house churches for the whole nation.

The strategy was the reverse of the DAWN approach of mobilizing the leadership from the top down. Instead, Mission 21 India provides training and materials for hundreds of denominations, missions and local churches. This means, of course, that the statistics they report probably overlap with those groups reporting their data to the CONS researchers. Still, the magnitude of what is being reported is considerable.

To find out how the project was doing since its inception in 1985, ten well-trained researchers were sent into the field for a six-month period. They came back with impressive numbers. Their survey showed that 18,963 "Witnessing Prayer Cells" or house churches were planted by 1,535 graduates of their program. These graduates reported starting 10,653 of these house churches while they were in training and 8,310 in subsequent years. On the other hand, 1,772 of the Witnessing Prayer Cells had disbanded by the time of the survey. This represents a failure rate of 9 percent of the 18,963 house churches.

It was also discovered that 100 percent of the graduates were receiving their total income from within India. Only 79 of the 795 church buildings that had been erected were financed at least in part by funds from the West.

This original survey failed to include a question about how many new churches were then planted by the pastors the graduates themselves had trained. In one case, it was accidentally learned that one graduate reported starting five house churches, but did not report that lay-people he trained planted another 25! This sent them back to another survey where a conservative estimate based on hard data from a sample group led them to conclude that an additional 68,000 house churches had been started, giving them a total of about 87,000.

"Based on the results of the survey," says John DeVries, president of Mission India, "we feel that the goal of planting 1,000 new house churches in each of the 850 MPU's for a total of 850,000 over a ten-year period is realistic."

"Yes, but are they reaching Hindus?" I can still hear my dear friend and mentor Dr. Donald McGavran asking this question every time I talked about church planting in India. In response, DeVries says that "about 95 percent of the converts come from the pagan world of Hindus and even some from Islam.

"Furthermore," he adds, "these are full churches in every New Testament sense. I believe this must be one of the largest saturation church planting movements in the world today. God is doing something unheard of and incredible that for some reason is not known throughout the Evangelical world."[1]

The day of the Holy Spirit

Elmer Kilbourne, a fourth generation missionary to Asia, feels the same way. He says that after retirement from 40 years of seeing fantastic growth in Korea, India was the last place he wanted to go. Still, the Lord led him there and gave him the vision of putting up 1,000 church buildings. (The full story will be related in Chapter Nine.)

Now, you couldn't drag him away. "I preached one day in Korea when we baptized 3,000," he told a group of us in a recorded interview. "I thought something like that would never happen again. But after two years in India I was in a service where we baptized 2,062 people." He says there is not a place in India—and he has traveled from one end to the other—where he could not start a church.

"India is the best kept secret in the world," he said. "It used to be a country that was one of the most resistant mission fields. After 200 years of missionary endeavor beginning with William Carey himself, there was little fruit. It was so discouraging that most traditional denominations pulled out.

"But I believe this is the day of the Holy Spirit. What we have seen in the last 10 years I don't think we could have seen in the prior ten. Even today people won't believe what God is doing in India.

"I met a veteran missionary to India the other day and

she said, 'Why do you lie about what is going on? What you claim is impossible.' This ignorance of what God is doing breaks my heart."

Believing Satan's lie

Another such voice comes from Indian evangelist S. D. Ponraj.

"I first met you nine years ago this week when you were teaching us in Madras," he told me in a recent visit to the Dawn Ministries office. "It was that week I caught the vision and committed my life to saturation church planting and one million churches for India."

So far, so good. But had he done anything about it in the intervening years? He had. He had taken leadership in developing the DAWN movement in India, he had held seminars all over the nation, and he had written and published books in three languages on the subject.

"We now have 2,000 missionaries from South India already in place in the Hindu belt in the North," he said. "Next week I will be back in India for the first of ten training sessions for these missionaries. Each one will be equipped and expected to train 25 church planters who will each be expected to plant five churches."

Let's see. That's 2,000 times 25 times five. A goal of 250,000 churches in just the next five years! More than doubling the total number of churches in all India! Through just this one ministry!

He explained that the Church in India and mission societies around the world had swallowed a lie of Satan. "He has used our leaders to convince us that the 700 million Hindus of North India are an impenetrable block.

"The reality is much different. It is only 20 percent of this population that is truly Hindu. These are the ones who have been reached with the gospel. Ghandi is an example of how they accepted the teachings of Jesus but rejected the person of Jesus.

"The other 560 million are not and never have been Hindu. They were told they were Hindus by the minority rulers and forced into the caste system, of which they naturally were put at the bottom. They are more and more open to the gospel. It is the day of the Holy Spirit for these millions."

Other top Indian scholars and mission leaders are saying the same thing. Among them are Dr. Victor Chaudhrie, world famous surgeon and former Dean of a large hospital and university; Ebenezer Sunder Raj, General Secretary of the India Missions Association; and Dr. Devanayagan, a scholar of the Dalits in India.[2] Their studies indicate there are up to 640 million native Indians of mostly Dravidian origin who have never been and never will be Hindus. Rather, they say, they were proclaimed to be Hindus by the stroke of the pen through several government censuses taken earlier in this century.

According to these men, the "forward" or "upper class" Hindus at that time required all Indians to specify whether they were Muslim, Christian, Jain or Sikh. If they checked none of these, they were automatically counted as Hindus!

They observe that for literally hundreds of millions of these artificially converted "low-caste" or "Dalit" Hindus, there now seems to be a new search for religious and cultural identity. Tired of being thought of as "doormats of the nation," many are beginning to see Christianity offering them a sense of individual value and dignity and even perhaps a way out of their low caste status.

These evangelical leaders say that a number of Dalit leaders are now asking for the right of the Dalits to choose their own religion without being socially ostracized by the 15 percent religious minority that greatly benefits from the status quo.

In a recent conference in India, for example, Dr. Devanayagan said, "We should get ready to become the catalyst for a massive movement to Christ in the next few years. We...need to be available to help our Indian people in their decision-making process which involves whole villages, people groups, tribes, clans and families."[3]

Back to the real world

Though this is a fascinating viewpoint and the above stories might seem almost incredible, none of this is intended to imply that we can now consider the job done in India. The statistics *are* daunting, the task *is* formidable. The mostly Indian speakers at the 1995 Congress acknowledged this.

Still, the 1,000 or so delegates heard reports of people groups turning to Christ. They were reminded that there are churches in every one of the 514 districts of the 25 states and seven regions of India. And even if only .15 percent of the people in the Hindi belt are believers, that still translates into 1,000,000 Christians! If God would have spared wicked Sodom and Gomorrah for *ten* righteous, what can he do, and what does he want to do, with one million who have been made righteous by the blood of the Lord Jesus Christ?

Knowing the difficulty first hand, virtually *every* speaker in the Second CONS Congress affirmed the vision of a church in every village and city neighborhood—a total of one million congregations—as a goal they were committed to and a goal that could be reached.

"There is no question but that the time is ripe for India," said Gupta at the close of the congress. "Our people are ready to turn to Christ. We must reach the winnable while they are still winnable."

DAWN and the remaining 70 percent

We rejoice in all the Lord is doing in India, our nation of entry into the world of unreached peoples. Still, we recognize another 70 percent of all unreached peoples are outside these borders. Where do we go from here?

Another 30 percent or so can be found in the other massive nation of the world, the land of China.

For years I have been saying that by far the best "DAWN" project in the world with the greatest "John Knoxer" is in the nation of China. I was referring, of course, to the vast multiplication of house churches that we can only say have come about under the prompting of the Holy Spirit. He himself was driving out the forces that had before now made something like this impossible.

While it is unrealistic even to think of mobilizing the Church of China for a classic DAWN congress such as we saw in the chapter on England, that does not mean the ball game is over.

As Roy Wingerd is quoted in Chapter Four, "The primary outcome of a DAWN congress is to get ownership by responsible leaders of the SCP vision and commitment to a certain number of churches to be planted by a certain date. This can happen by personal contact with such leaders one by one or two by two."

Though this obviously is a more difficult route in some respects, Wingerd is of the opinion that such an approach is within our grasp. He is in contact with DAWN-minded leaders that have the infrastructure to make this vision a reality for China.

Furthermore, there is a DAWN project of sorts already underway. I learned of this only when I sat down in the Hong Kong office of Kenneth Lo when on my way to the Fifth DAWN Philippine Congress outside Manila. What a surprise when Lo, who serves as Hong Kong Director for the Far East Broadcast Company, pulled out a full-color brochure promoting the DAWN China project! It was already underway! A national goal had already been set: *One million more churches in China by AD 2000!*

The Far East Broadcasting Company (FEBC) beams about 40 broadcast hours a day into many regions and many languages of China. But on January 1, 1994, they began two additional 15-minute "DAWN China" broadcasts and planned to follow this with a daily 30-minute training program for church multiplication.

These broadcasts communicate the DAWN vision and cover such topics as Discipleship Training, Personal Evangelism, Evangelism and Church Planting, Church Growth, Missions and others. Rev. Lo is also working with two other organizations in developing DAWN China. They have already sent booklets throughout the Mainland to teach the principles of DAWN and church multiplication. Several months after my visit, we received reports from Lo of individual churches being started here and there and some church multiplication projects underway.

"Even if we reach the goal," says Lo, "China's Church will only represent 11.59 percent of the projected population of 1,294,000,000. We are asking believers everywhere to pray that the Christians in China will even more greatly endeavor to evangelize and plant churches. Our gospel broadcasts will assist in this project."

Lo, of course, is really sticking his neck out. Mainland China officials certainly know about the ministry of FEBC and now, through radio and printed materials, about the DAWN idea. Lo realizes they don't like it at all. But while some pastors are leaving Hong Kong because of its reversion to China in 1997, Lo is determined not only to stay but to see that his fellow countrymen on the mainland will be reached for Christ.

Just as I'm finishing this manuscript another news item hit my desk that reports an estimated 20,000 "radio churches" have been started in China over the past two years by Trans World Radio and a partner agency, China Ministry International. Their goal is for 40,000 such churches by the end of 1996.[4]

Good news from the world of Islam

Though in a different setting and under entirely different circumstances, DAWN is catching on in the hearts, minds and plans amongst leaders in the Arab and Muslim world as well. Dawn Ministries missionaries Steve Steele and Wolfgang Fernández are in close contact with projects developing in at least five of these nations. Others are showing interest. We also consider Don McCurry of Ministries to Muslims and Wolfgang Simson of Dawn Europa as part of our team for reaching this part of the world. Some of the stories and openings they report are almost unbelievable.

Actually, the first DAWN-like project within what has become popularized as the 10/40 window goes back to the early 1970's. While the Lord was taking me step by step through a process that would lead to the DAWN strategy in the Philippines, God was also speaking to Chris Marantika in Indonesia. Without being aware of each other, Marantika was developing what became his One, One, One project. This envisioned one church being planted in each one village in one generation of this nation with the largest Muslim population in the world. Though there has been great opposition, churches continue to be multiplied in Muslim communities throughout the land.[5]

It is too early and too dangerous to put many of the stories and plans for Muslim nations in print. Still, we can see again that God himself is driving out the forces of evil that have kept multitudes of hidden peoples of the world out of the range of the gospel. These nations too can be filled with the knowledge of the glory of the Lord, can be saturated with cells of believers in the living God.

South Korea points the way

There will be different and ingenious ways to go about this in each Muslim nation and other unreached people groups. The plan the Church in South Korea has for their fraternal nation to the North won't work everywhere, but it is a sample of creativity that can challenge and inspire others in their particular situations.

In April of 1995 our son, Len, and his trumpet trio, Gabriel Brass, represented the United States in a music festival in Pyongyang, North—yes, *North*—Korea. In probable thanks to Jimmy Carter, this was only the second year that musicians were invited from the U.S. to participate with about 40 mainly communist or former communist nations in this annual event.

After experiencing the oppressive atmosphere of North Korea, Len says that stopping in Beijing, China, on the way home was like being back in Los Angeles by comparison. Almost any public evidence of Christianity that previously flourished in the North had been stamped out.

On Easter Sunday, they were taken to two "showcase" churches. In both situations they were told that it was too bad they had not been at the "earlier service where about 200 attended." In actuality, there were about 20 in one and maybe a dozen in the other. Even these "worshippers" leafed through song books and gazed around the building as if the atmosphere was totally strange to them.

Near the end of the second service, the soprano soloist with the trio sang that wonderful hymn, "How Great Thou Art." As she did, an old Korean woman stood, her face aglow with faith and joy, and in English sang along with her. Len and his friends wept. In all of North Korea, there was at least one genuine believer.

How many more are there? No one knows, of course, but North Korea seems as much an unreached people and nation as any could be. What to do in a situation like that?

The South Korean Church has an answer. After one of his many trips to Korea before the Global Consultation on World Evangelization in Seoul in 1995, AD2000 International Director Luis Bush reported on the readiness of the Korean Church to tackle the responsibility of discipling their nation to the North. He told me that they have caught the saturation-church-planting vision and have a thrilling plan. They do not expect to be caught unprepared for the time when North Korea opens or is unified with South Korea.

Bush said that according to Kang Hee Ahn, the challenge has gone out to enlist one million Christians to each adopt and pray for one of the 4,300 districts of North Korea. Their vision is that 100,000 students will form into teams and take one- or two-year breaks from their collegiate studies to live in the districts they have prayed for. While there, they will serve the communities, evangelize *and work towards their goal of planting more than 30,000 churches!* This would give them more than one church for every 1,000 people in the country.

As of November, 1993, more than 40,000 students had already committed themselves!

As Peter Wagner wrote in *Spreading the Fire*,[6] "Many believe that if the Iron Curtain could come down, as it did, with such little previous warning, a series of similar events over the next few years could radically change the political landscape of the world and topple some of the most formidable traditional barriers to the gospel."

Are we ready?

The question of this book is, when and as this happens, will the Church be similarly ready to move in with an effective strategy that will quickly fill newly opened nations and people groups with cells of committed believers, with Spirit-filled and Spirit-led congregations?

While this seems to be "the day of the Holy Spirit," in at least some of the great unreached mission fields of the world, this does not seem to be the case in what has been one of the great sending nations of the world in this century. Just what *are* we going to do with the slumbering Church in the United States?

[1] *DAWN REPORT*, December, 1993 and April, 1994.

[2] Wolfgang Simson, *Internet*, April 20, 1995, an e-mail service: 100337,2106.

[3] Ibid.

[4] "China: 'Radio Churches,'" *Pulse*, May 3, 1996, p.3.

[5] The full story of this movement is recorded in *DAWN 2000: 7 Million Churches to Go*, pp.17-18, 68, 161-162.

[6] C. Peter Wagner, (Ventura, CA: Regal Books, 1994), p.70.

Chapter Eight

USA: "Last of the Giants"

'America will not be won to Christ by establishing more churches like the vast majority of those we now have.'

Charles Chaney
President, Southern Baptist Home Mission Board

Speaking from the viewpoint of a North American, I believe we continue to have an essential role in world revival and completion of the Great Commission. Though we are rather anemic at the moment, the potential is there. We may be one of the "last of the giants"—to steal the title of George Otis, Jr's. book—to experience revival and get on board with the movement for discipling whole nations. But when we do, good things will happen.

Activity? Yes. Results? No!

But we're not there yet. Consider this. There are around 375,000 Protestant churches in our land, many tens of thousands of which are evangelical and/or charismatic in nature. Every year we spend *billions* of dollars on evangelical activities. We have hundreds of evangelical Bible schools and seminaries. There are more than 6,000 Bible book stores throughout the nation. Almost any time of the day or night one can find a gospel program on radio or TV.

And despite the accelerating leftward drift in our culture, we are still the most open society in the world.

Still, according to W. Charles Arn of Church Growth, Inc.,[1] in not a single one of our 3,141 counties did church attendance increase at a rate faster than general population growth during the whole *decade* of the 1980's. We are barely winning enough of our children to the Lord plus an occasional outsider to keep the Church from actual decline.

Furthermore, the Church with all its resources seems to have little impact on a culture in free fall. While we have been getting on each other's nerves in our evangelical ghettos, look what has happened outside our walls. Comparing the 1960's with the 1990's, Bill Bennett in *The Index Of Leading Cultural Indicators* shares some very painful statistics. During those years when the population increased by just 41 percent, there has been a 500 percent increase in violent crimes; more than a 400 percent increase in illegitimate births; a quadrupling in divorces; a tripling of the percentage of children living in single parent homes; more than a 200 percent increase in teenage suicide rate. By the year 2000, he says, 40 percent of all U.S. births and 80 percent of minority births will occur out of wedlock.[2]

Our record makes a mockery of our theological beliefs. We no longer represent a powerful force either in our Jerusalem and Judea—among home-grown Americans,—in our Samaria—among all those cultural groups that have migrated to our shores—, nor yet in the uttermost parts of the earth among those *still* unreached peoples.

No amount of political awareness and action, though good in itself, is going to bail us out. No amount of cosmetic changes in how we do church or missions is going to be sufficient. What we must call on the Lord for is a mega revival that will arrest the attention of the whole Church in America, that will bring us to our knees in heart-wrenching repentance and lift us up in newness of life to powerfully re-evangelize our nation and take our share of responsibility for the rest of the world.

Needed: A profound paradigm shift

This next thrust, which is already beginning to emerge, will require the profound paradigm shift from "inside-out" thinking to "outside-in" thinking, from simple "church growth" to "church multiplication." We will have to change our frame of reference from just increasing the size of our own little turf and begin making plans for the discipling of whole cities, counties, states, regions and, ultimately, the whole nation. This will call for the whole Body of Christ in these geographical entities uniting in the vision of filling them with growing cells of believers capable of impacting their whole environments.

I recognize, however, that church planting, let alone church *multiplication*, is a hard sell in America among many pastors, denomination heads and even among some national Church leaders. Such is not the case with Larry Lewis, President of the Southern Baptist Home Mission Board.

"Some people say I am obsessed with church starting," he said in a message delivered to several thousand pastors and home missionaries in a denominational convention in 1991.[3] "The truth is, the only effective, fruitful way to evangelize this nation and minister to its needs is through the New Testament Church. We start churches not to reach some goal or fulfill some campaign, but to evangelize this nation and minister to its needs.

"Our real goal," he continued, "is to see to it that no human being could be born and live and die in these United States and territories who has not had the gospel clearly proclaimed to him, who has not had opportunity to lay hold of the promises of salvation through Jesus Christ, who has not had opportunity to become part of a vital, Bible-witnessing, ministering congregation of people.

"The hardest job in your life," Lewis concluded, "will be

to convince me we already have too many churches. When our research department tells me that we now have 172 million lost people in America, that we have more unsaved and unchurched people than we've ever had in the history of this nation, you'll have a hard time convincing me that the day is over when we need to begin new congregations."

To the voice of Larry Lewis could be added many scholars and practitioners. James Engel and Wilbert Norton, who years ago wrote the book *What's Gone Wrong with the Harvest?*, said that one demonstrated principle of church growth is that the only way for a Christian movement to make gains in a given society is by the multiplication of new churches. "Multiplication of new congregations of believers," they wrote, "is the normal and expected output of a healthy body." [4]

Charles Chaney, Vice President of Southern Baptist Home Mission Board, quotes the great missiologist Donald McGavran who observed that "The multiplication of soundly Christian churches throughout all segments of society, throughout all homogenous units, till every people, every ethnic unit is seeded with churches is...a procedure well pleasing to God."[5]

Four major challenges

How can we transfer this challenge and vision to the Church of America? For our part, we were greatly blessed in Dawn Ministries when the Lord led Jack Dennison to join our small staff of missionaries as North America Regional Coordinator. His sense of calling as well as his experience as military chaplain, pastor, seminary professor (Multnomah) in church growth and chairman of a united effort called Northwest Harvest combined to give him the ideal background for encouraging a national strategy for the USA project to be brought into being.

After becoming thoroughly acquainted with the DAWN

strategy and then meeting with key leaders in virtually every region of the nation, Dennison has concluded there are at least four challenges facing the Church in America in a revived effort to complete the discipling of the peoples of our cities.

"In the **first** place," writes Dennison in a paper privately circulated, "the Church in America is currently unprepared for a revival movement of God."

By way of illustration, he refers to what has become known as "The Miracle of Modesto" mentioned in Chapter One. Dennison emphasizes not so much the miracle of 35,000 people turning to Christ in an eight-week period—truly astounding in itself—but the tragedy of its early demise.

"Can you imagine praying for revival, as we all are, and then deliberately stopping it when it comes?" he writes. "That is exactly what happened in Modesto. The Church was so overwhelmed by the sheer number of people coming to Christ that they chose to discontinue the drama presentation that God was using as the fuel behind the revival. They were not able to incorporate this great influx of new converts.

"The time to get ready for revival is now. We simply cannot say with integrity that we believe that revival is impending and continue business as usual."

Dennison's **second** point is that "We do not have enough seats in our existing churches to accommodate a revival movement of God."

He describes a common phenomenon in nearly every city of America. "If every person who claimed to be Christian showed up for church on the same day," he observes, "there would be no room for anyone else."

An example of this is found right here in Colorado Springs, one of the more conservative and evangelical cities of the whole nation. Research by our Dawn team indicates that 35 percent of the residents are found on a church membership *roll*, but only 22 percent of the population can be found in attendance on a given Sunday. If all those on the church roll showed up for services on a particular Sunday there would be seating capacity for no more than 4 percent of the unchurched population. Clearly, we are unprepared for a movement of God in our city.

In another situation, one of our missionaries was told by leaders of the Church in Anchorage, Alaska, that they had been praying for revival for ten years. Some simple arithmetic, however, showed that there were currently very few seats available in their churches if revival did come. They prayed for something that they were totally unprepared to handle.

"I wonder if there is a message for us in 2 Kings 4," asks Dennison. "The widow approached Elisha because the creditors were about to foreclose on her home and enslave her children. Elisha instructed her to go home and get every jar she could find. You know the story: as long as there were empty vessels, God filled them. As soon as all vessels were full, however, the flow stopped. How is God going to fill the vessels of our churches with the new wine of revival when they are already too few and too full?"

In the **third** place, Dennison says that "This problem of vacancy is compounded by the cultural distance between the church and those coming to Christ today."

He continues by saying that "The cultural environment in the majority of our churches is so foreign, uncomfortable and uninviting to the converts of today that it actually repels rather than attracts people to the church."

Charles Chaney, the Southern Baptist Church leader whose goal it is to reach 50,000 congregations by the year 2000, has arrived at a similar conclusion. "America will not be won to Christ by existing churches," he says, "even if they should suddenly become vibrantly and evangelistically alive. Nor will the United States be won to Christ by establishing more churches like the vast majority of those we now have...."[6]

Both of these observers of the Church throughout our nation agree that the church culture in the majority of our congregations will not change. They will therefore remain an impenetrable barrier for most new converts looking for a church home. The pre-World War II generation, for example, is largely incapable of effectively reaching the boomer generation. The churches that are able to reach boomers do not appeal to the busters.

"Just these three generations that exist in our society today are more culturally different from one another than they have ever been in the history of mankind," says Dennison. "This is a phenomenon that revival has never before been faced with. Needed are culturally appropriate churches for each new generation of converts that is structured to address its needs and stylistic preferences."

Dennison suggests that perhaps 80 percent of the 375,000 churches in America are plateaued or declining primarily because they have lost their connection with and their ability to identify with and influence the people and culture around them. New wineskins are needed for the new wine of revival.

Dennison gives another reason for believing that thousands of churches of a new kind are required for the discipling of our cities. It takes into account that we don't have the finances or the land for a fraction of these needed churches. Zoning laws in most cities are becoming more and more restrictive.

"If we are going to evangelize and congregationalize each new generation of believers," he says, "we need to broaden our definition of 'church' and legitimize new models. We need multi-congregational churches, satellite churches, cell-churches, house churches and other viable models to be embraced by our denominations and parachurch groups. We must begin with the location and needs of the convert in mind."

What if, as Bill Bright suggests, 25 million Americans turn to Christ in the next five years as he expects to happen just through Campus Crusade ministries alone? Just for those converts we would need 125,000 new churches with the same average membership of 194 people that we currently have.

"We need many more churches," concludes Dennison, "but we can no longer support facility-based church models as the only way, or even the best way, to congregationalize America."

The **fourth** challenge that Dennison sees "is that of reaching ethnic America."

Virtually every race, every people, every ethnic group in the world can be found in the United States. When revival comes, many people from foreign lands will carry the Spirit of God back to their countries of origin. One aspect of the strategic role the U.S. Church continues to play in world evangelization is discipling the many ethnic groups living in the mission field of our own backyards.

In Portland, Oregon, there are more than 100 ethnic groups, most of which remain unreached or under-evangelized. The 100,000-member Hispanic community has only 1 percent of its population attending a Protestant Church.

Houston, Texas, alone has more Vietnamese than any whole state in the union but one. There are 44,000 Filipinos in Las Vegas, 40,000 Hmong in Fresno, 34,000 Chinese in St. Louis. In the Dallas school system, a total of 94 different language groups are represented. Currently, according to researcher George Barna, 32 million people in America speak some language other than English as their primary language.

The inner city of America has become home to countless numbers of ethnic groups including a large percentage of the nations Afro-American, Hispanic and other major ethnic populations. What can be said of the Church's effectiveness in reaching these people living in these places?

Again I quote Charles Chaney: "The rise of the great city is one of the most important sociological developments of the nineteenth century. Urbanization has continued to sweep across the North American continent throughout the twentieth century. An unquestioned axiom of twentieth-century Christian historiography is that the Protestant churches have lost the cities of the continent."[7]

We have abandoned the inner city of America. The church of the inner city, primarily a church of color, ministers on territory abandoned by others, given up on by past generations of white Christians.

African-American author William Pannell states that "The evangelical church in the suburbs has virtually no comprehension of the hopelessness that abounds in this needy mission field just a couple of dozen miles away. Nevertheless, it sees itself as called to proclaim the gospel to all people and to translate the values of the Judeo-Christian heritage into all levels of the culture."[8]

He says there is a sense in which the phrase "evangelicals in the city" is an oxymoron, a contradiction of terms. Ethnic America is one of our greatest challenges and opportunities. As one Christian leader has flatly said, "If we fail to reach ethnic America, we will miss America."

The simple conclusion from these four factors that Dennison points out is that we need many more churches if we are going to provide a church for every person in every ethnic, geographic, cultural and sociological grouping of people in America.

For this task, each American city needs to have a plan in place, that if successful, would lead directly to the discipling of the whole city by filling every piece of its cultural mosaic with vibrant cells of believers.

Is America getting ready for DAWN?

By God's grace, I am of a mind to believe that the adage "It is always darkest before the dawn" applies to America.

That our miserable record of recent decades is about to be transformed. That the revival being experienced in some parts will at last, as an "untimely birth," reach the shores of America. Hand in hand with this revival will be the beginning of another major thrust in the discipling—or rediscipling—of this nation.

We have the story, for instance, of Dr. Henry Lyons, Chairman of the National Baptist Convention. His denomination of eight million members represents one out of every four of the 32 million black persons in this country. He was scheduled to meet with Dawn missionaries Jack Dennison and Steve and Mike Steele for a two-hour meeting in the Denver airport. The late arrival of Lyon's flight, however, left them just 25 minutes to talk before Lyons had to leave for a press conference with the mayor of the city.

After a brief explanation of DAWN, Dennison and Steele quickly got to the point: "Is God the Holy Spirit calling the African-American Church in America to complete the task of discipling the African-American nation within our country?" they asked Lyons.

He had just five minutes to reply. "There is a coming together of the Black Church like we have never seen before," he said. "The African-American Church has begun to be joined together in one spirit. They are ripe and ready; their fears are waylaid; they are experiencing a unity not seen before.

"Two weeks ago at our convention in Birmingham, Alabama," he continued, "the Holy Spirit fell on me and issued a call to my life to challenge the Black Church to evangelize the Black community of America. I did what the Holy Spirit told me to do.

"But when I went back to my room I confessed to the Lord that I did not know how to do it! Two weeks later I am sitting in a conference room at the Denver airport and realize that *you are the answer to my prayer. You are telling me how to do it.* I have been restless these last several days and unable to sleep well in anticipation of this meeting and now I know why."

That is not the only good news for a possible DAWN-type project for America. Now the Hispanics are also on board! In November, 1995, Mike Steele and Berna Salcedo of Dawn Ministries attended the Hispanic Evangelical Ministry Association (AMEN) in Long Beach, California. They met with key leaders from almost all the Hispanic regions of the U.S. as a followup to a process that had begun earlier that year. In two days, these leaders agreed to develop the DAWN strategy and named it "Hispanics For Christ: a church within easy reach of every Hispanic." At that time, the first Hispanic DAWN-type congress was scheduled for 1997 to be held in Portland, Oregon, for the Northwest region of the country. Other regional congresses would follow.

It is noteworthy that the Southern Baptists under the leadership of Bob Sena already have 3,847 Hispanic churches. They could easily double that number and provide another 4,000 Hispanic congregations in five years from just this one denomination.

There are even indications that the Church of the rest of the country is getting ready for an all-out united effort. Though at this time not committed to making church-multiplication its primary goal, Mission America, headed by Paul Cedar, shows promise for taking one city at a time. Another effort by a consortium of 15 denominations, most of the largest ones in the nation, is also coming together for united city-wide efforts. This group *is* making church planting its central focus.

From the looks of things, DAWN USA could well emerge as a great conflagration from the moving together of many smaller fires. Perhaps there will be many ethnic DAWN-type projects beyond those already envisioned for Hispanics and blacks. The denominational thrusts into cities hold great promise. In addition to this are the fellowships of pastors getting together for prayer that are beginning to move on to the next step of developing strategic plans.

As these continue to burn brightly and spread, their convergence could well be a part of—if not actually usher in—the revival fire so desperately needed and is quite possibly on the way.

"Come over and help *US*!"

I have been writing this chapter to North Americans and as a North American myself. I do have two final things to say to everyone else, however.

One, please, please, heed the Macedonian call and come over and help us, "us" as in "U.S." For 200 years we have sent our sons and daughters to pioneer, to sacrifice and many times to die in order to bring the glorious gospel to you. I know you appreciate it. Now the time has come for you to return the favor. We need you.

With your language skills and cultural affinity, come help us reach the very responsive 25 million Hispanics in our land. With your understanding and experience of persecution and depravation, come help us reach 30 million African Americans. With your burden for the unreached peoples of the world, come help us reach the growing number of Muslims, Chinese and East Indians that have come to our shores. We need your help in bringing the gospel to the East Europeans, the Asians, the Arabs and scores of other peoples that have come to the one place in the world where they are most likely to hear and respond to the gospel. Come open our eyes to our incredible neglect of the half million foreign students in our midst. These potential leaders, more than half of whom come from unreached peoples of the 10/40 window, can be brought to the Lord and sent back to prepare their nations for the coming of the gospel and the multiplication of congregations in their lands.

Come, show us how to reach our own neighbors, friends and relatives. We don't even know how to do that anymore.

But hurry! Every year thousands of foreigners return to their native lands without Christ or become so enamored with the American life-style that they lose sight of their spiritual needs. We're nowhere near getting the job done. We need your help.

Come show us your deep, abiding life in Christ. Let us see and catch the warmth and joy of your walk with the Lord. Show us what it means to pray and persist and sacrifice until converts are won, are gathered into vibrant cells of believers, are equipped and sent out to be witnesses and pioneer missionaries.

Two, pray for us. I know you are praying, urgently praying, for your own nations and for the unreached peoples of the world. We also are in desperate need of your prayer.

Pray that the strongholds in our land will be broken. That we will be loosed from the chains of apathy, detestable lukewarmness, ignorance of what God is doing in the world, intellectual pride, preoccupation with the host of things that keep us busy but unproductive and unfulfilled. Pray for our deliverance from all those things that keep us from seeing and having concern for all those in our midst who are lost and without hope in this world or the world to come.

And pray for revival in our land. No doubt there is urgent need to break strongholds in America, in your land and throughout the world. But what if we cast out all demons only to find each returns to a clean house with seven more so that the last condition is worse than before? (Mt. 12:43-45).

Pray, rather, that a revived Church will be so quickened and renewed that it will be ready for a massive response to the gospel, that it will be prepared to make a church available to every convert in every small community of mankind in America and in the world. Pray into existence in every nation and people group the implementation of this saturation church planting strategy for the end of the age and pray until Jesus comes on the clouds of the sky, with power and great glory....to gather his elect from the four winds, from one end of the heavens to the other" (Mt. 24:30, 31).

Now is the time for the Body of Christ worldwide to perceive itself as a body and begin to function as a body. Nothing less is going to be adequate to capitalize on the world revival that is on its way and in some form already here.

---

[1]"Leadership Journal," Spring, 1996, p.75.

[2]*The Index* is published by Empower America, Washington D.C.; quoted in "The Pastor's Weekly Briefing," Vol. 3, No. 18, by H. B. London, Focus on the Family, Colorado Springs, CO.

[3]"A Church for Every Swarm," in DAWN Report, December, 1991, p.4.

[4]James F. Engel and Wilbert Norton, *What's Gone Wrong with the Harvest?* (Grand Rapids, MI: Zondervan Publishing House, 1975), p.143-144.

[5] Charles Chaney, *Church Planting at the End of the Twentieth Century* (Wheaton, IL: Tyndale House Publishers), p.60.

[6]Ibid., p.4.

[7]Ibid., p.89.

[8]William Pannell, *The Coming Race Wars?* (Grand Rapids, MI: Zondervan Publishing House, 1993), p.116.

Part III

The End of the Age

Chapter Nine

Western Missions in Crisis

'If reality mirrors the image, then we, the U.S. missionary movement, are in a crisis of earth shaking proportions.'

Paul McKaughan
President and CEO of EFMA

The crisis we are facing in the Church of the United States undoubtedly is also a root cause for the crisis we are facing in the missions enterprise in North America.

In a brilliant paper delivered in April of 1994, Paul McKaughan, President of the Evangelical Fellowship of Mission Agencies (EFMA) in the United States, spoke of the Chinese pictogram for the word "crisis." He said this comes from merging the signs for "opportunity" and for "threat." In reference to the missionary movement in the United States, he listed many opportunities facing missions, but also many threats and potential pitfalls.

His conclusion was this: "I have suggested that in the Chinese pictogram for 'crisis' we see the clashing of opportunity and threat like the wave on the rocky seashore. If reality mirrors the image, then we, the U.S. missionary movement, are in a crisis of earth shaking proportions."

Not content with mere analysis, McKaughan is leading the Board of EFMA in a multi-year search for solutions for the looming crisis. Since it is my privilege and opportunity to serve on that board, I too have been wrestling with the question of the survival of the North American missions enterprise. At least four things occur to me.

One, we must do more than tinker with the machinery. As Larry Walker, Southwest Regional Director for the Association of Church Missions Committees, says, "We must not merely do missions *better,* we must do missions *differently.*"

Two, I believe it won't be until the Church in the U.S. experiences a powerful Holy Spirit awakening and breaks loose from its lethargy for evangelism and church multiplication into tens of thousands of unchurched communities at home that overseas frontier missions will again strike fire throughout the land.

We have experienced this phenomenon in a number of DAWN projects around the world. Many times it isn't until the Church in a nation experiences the exhilaration of multiplying congregations in its own land that it gets excited about neighboring and distant lands as well.

Three, it appears virtually to all of us on the EFMA Board that the missions community has a role, if not an obligation, to help bring about this renewal in the U.S. Church. We can no longer be content with asking churches for their money and their sons and daughters for missions overseas. Both for the sake of making a disciple of our own nation as well as the missions challenge abroad, we must become involved at a deeper level at home.

What this help will look like is not clear, though one idea is perhaps worth mentioning. It takes into account that there are probably more former missionaries in the U.S. than current missionaries on the field. With their cross-cultural and language experience, could these not be mobilized to partner with denominations and local churches in evangelizing and discipling into new and existing congregations the host of ethnics that populate our cities and even our countryside?

I address some of the above three issues elsewhere in the book, but will in this chapter take a longer look at a fourth issue relating to the survival and health of the North American missions enterprise. The message will not surprise you!

Four, there is need for a massive paradigm shift in how we go about doing missions both in the "reached" and "unreached" areas of the world. It is the shift, suggested by this whole book, to thinking in terms of completing the task through a vast multiplication of local congregations until "...the earth (is filled) with the knowledge of the glory of the Lord" (Hab. 2:14). It is a shift from doing missions as usual to a mentality of actually completing the Great Commission in our time. It is a shift to imaging the consummation of the age and what it will take in real terms to bring it about.

It would be presumptuous of me to suggest exactly what shape this paradigm shift should take in any particular mission society or on any particular field. As a missions observer and reporter, however, I can relate some models others have developed and then at the end of the chapter make a brief suggested list of things to look at. Mind you, I'm not talking about the nuts and bolts of how to run a mission agency, but rather the overall vision of what it will take to complete the Great Commission and the most direct role Western missions can play in this.

An *evangelist* catches the idea

Mike Downey, whose first contact with Dawn Ministries was at the Global Consultation on World Evangelization in Korea in May of 1995, is one who has embraced this paradigm shift with a vengeance. Even in Korea he only met Steve Steele, our CEO, because he needed to borrow a laptop computer. Before that, he had never heard of the DAWN strategy or of Dawn Ministries.

Incredibly, six months later he and Curtis Hail, his Executive Vice President, flew up from Dallas to our Colorado Springs office just to meet with Steve and me for a couple of hours.

From the moment Mike burst into my office exuding energy from every pore, I could see that here was not a mild-mannered professor type who had come to the same conclusions through hours of contemplation in an ivory tower. No, here was a zealot with revolution on his mind!

"What Martin Luther was to the Roman Catholic Church," he said when we were well into the interview, "we are attempting for the modern missions movement. We want to launch a reformation that will put the Great Commission back into the hands of the so-called laity by mobilizing millions of them to fill every nation and people group with vibrant, evangelizing congregations of believers."

He was certainly singing our song, but he wasn't through. "By the year 2020," he said later, "it is projected there will be nine billion people on planet Earth. We want to work with dozens of denominations around the world to see nine million churches by then. One for every 1,000 people. So we only need nine million lay people—men and women who want nothing more in all of life than to reach the world for Christ. That's all it will take. Such a small number!"

Breathtaking! In an instant, Mike Downey made our mission statement look anemic by comparison: "The purpose of Dawn Ministries is to see saturation church planting become the generally accepted and fervently practiced strategy for completing the Great Commission in our time."

This is where Mike Downey is now, but it is not where he began. The process by which he made this paradigm shift is both a fascinating story of how God leads as well as another affirmation that the DAWN vision is not made in the USA but comes from the heart of God.

Downey grew up in a nominal Christian home, but didn't experience his own personal encounter with Christ until he was 16. "I knew then that I had found the answer I was so desperately searching for, trying to figure out the meaning of life," he related to us. "I am very grateful that I latched on to Christ and never let go."

That same year, he began dreaming "with my eyes open" about preaching the gospel and winning millions to Christ. He didn't have to wait long to take his first steps in that direction. For the following year, when Mike was only 17, his pastor of the 6,000-member Tallowood Baptist Church in Houston invited him to preach.

"I'm sure my sermon was pitiful," he told us, "but when I gave the invitation, people spontaneously started going from one side of the auditorium to the other, confessing their sin to one another. This lasted for 45 minutes. I hadn't even mentioned this in my message."

Finally, his pastor stood up and said, "Tonight, this is God's 'amen' that young Mike Downey is called by God to be a preacher of the gospel."

This was the beginning of a crusade ministry that in 1975 led to a preaching opportunity in Mexico during his senior year at Baylor University. "I was so profoundly impressed with the response and wonderful opportunity to reach people for Christ that I decided to go back after my graduation in 1976," he said.

He did, spending a year living with a Mexican family, becoming bi-lingual and "falling in love with the Hispanic people." This was not forgotten during the following years at Dallas Seminary where he spent his spare time doing door-to-door evangelism in a black housing community and preaching from a picnic table in a near-by park. He says emotionally he felt like a jackass, but a friend later reminded him that his world-wide ministry was based on the words of Jesus who said "He who is faithful in a very little is faithful also in much" (Lk. 16:10 RSV).

Much to his surprise, however, the path to this world-wide ministry did not take him either through missions or even through a crusade ministry. It began, rather, while pastoring in a small town in Oklahoma.

"In 1984 we called a Cuban evangelist to join our staff to start an Hispanic ministry," he said. "One of the first things Ramón Alemán did was take a team to Chihuahua, Mexico, to do evangelism in a new housing sub-division. There was such a wonderful response with several hundred receiving Christ that the church we were working with decided to start a daughter congregation in the area.

"Now it dawned on me that not only had hundreds come to Christ but that we had made a *permanent* contribution to the Kingdom. A new church had been started! 'Man,' I said, 'this is the missing link!'

"When we came back I was so excited from the experience that I said to the team, 'If this works so great, starting a new church accidentally, let's go back and start new churches on purpose.'"

That was the beginning of what became the vision of seeing to it that there would be nine million churches in the world by 2020. The next trip took them to Monterrey, Mexico, where three churches were planted instead of the one they had in mind. This was followed by a second trip to Monterrey where they shared the vision with about 25 pastors in the city. After a long wait for their response, an elderly, respected Baptist pastor stood and said, "My brothers, the voice of the Holy Spirit has spoken to these two men to help us win our city to Christ."

The church-planting campaign they implemented in 1986 resulted in 12 new congregations and 22 in the next campaign the following year.

Since his call to preach in 1970, Mike says he literally spent 17 years looking for the best strategy to complete the Great Commission. Now he had the answer.

"Number one," he says, "if you can put a church in every neighborhood of every city and town in the world, and that church will simply saturate their own back yard with the gospel, I tell you as the Lord God lives in heaven we will finish the Great Commission in our lifetime. Church planting is number one.

"Number two, the Great Commission will be fulfilled by a lay movement and I can prove it to you. There are currently 5.8 billion people in the world and about 250,000 vocational missionaries of every kind from Roman Catholics to Pentecostals. That's one for every 23,000 people! What we must do is mobilize millions of lay people not only to pray for missions, not only to give money to missions, but to roll up their sleeves and *do* missions."

Being a doer himself, Mike Downey founded Global Missions Fellowship in 1987. Since then, his society has grown to 60 full-time missionaries who have trained thousands of lay-people to plant over 1,000 churches in 48 countries.

This, of course, is a long way from his dream of nine million lay people planting nine million churches in the next 25 years. At least on paper, he's got that figured out as well.

"One of our distinctives," he explains, "is that we require each missionary that joins our staff to sign in blood—at least in spirit—that he will replicate himself a minimum of once a year, every year. That means enlisting and training another person to be a church-planting missionary who will take teams of lay people to plant churches.

"While this has not resulted in doubling every year, we have sustained a 47 percent Average Annual Growth Rate for the last seven years. This year we will grow by 60 percent and will be in about 50 countries. We expect to be in the 150 major nations of the world that include about 96 percent of the world's population within three years.

"God helping us, we hope to plant 400 churches in

1996, 800 in 1997, 1,600 the next year and then 3,200, 6,000, 12,000, 24,000 and so on in the years to follow."

While mathematically, at least, this could lead to the nine million churches all by itself in just 16 years, there are many obvious pitfalls, not the least of which are the formidable governmental and cultural barriers hindering the way to at least half the world's population.

Nevertheless, the dream, the goals, the plan and the actual working out of ministry are all in line with what the Lord is saying to other leaders around the world and in line with the paradigm shift that must take place to see the consummation of the age in our time.

An Alliance for SCP

While Global Missions Fellowship was started from scratch on this new set of paradigms, Dwight Smith tackled the much more difficult task of changing the direction of an aging society that had lost its way into a patchwork of field ministries.

Dwight's commitment to Saturation Church Planting was highly developed long before he took over as President of United World Mission in January, 1988. To the great credit of the board of UWM, Dwight was given free hand to turn the mission into a society devoted exclusively to the SCP concept. Under his energetic leadership, every aspect of the mission changed significantly. Their recruiting, training of new missionaries and retraining of those already on board, as well as their expectations of what was to be accomplished on the field, all revolved around the concept of planting church-planting churches until whole regions and nations were filled with them.

He and his mission were then quite ready for the massive SCP project that emerged from the Nations for Christ Congress that was held May 25-29, 1992, in Riga, Latvia. It was in this setting that about 800 delegates gathered from 15 nations just emerging from the 70-year nightmare of the communist Soviet Union.

Thomas Wang, who had been Executive Director of the Lausanne Movement and is now Chairman of the AD2000 and Beyond Movement, saw the potential for a great harvest among these newly liberated peoples. Teaming up with Pastor Joseph Bondarenko of the Mission of the Cross in Riga, Wang was determined to accomplish something more than just bringing about an outpouring of emotions for these leaders, most of whom had never had an opportunity to gather like this in their lifetimes.

So he asked Dawn Ministries to develop a followup program that would bring depth and continuation. Recognizing the enormity of the task, we in turn asked Smith and United World Mission to shoulder this responsibility.

In a relatively short period, Smith was able to mobilize and train about 50 expatriates who attended the Congress. These were divided into teams that returned with each of the national delegations to their homelands. The purpose was to determine whether or not these nations newly liberated from the communistic yoke were ready for a national saturation church planting strategy along the lines of DAWN.

When team members reported enough encouragement from leaders in these nations, Smith took responsibility for developing what became The Alliance for Saturation Church Planting.

The concept was to retrain and re-deploy teams of missionaries to pour into these nations while the opportunity was ripe and infuse them with the SCP idea. With a combined population of over 300 million, the vision was to see 300,000 total churches in the region, or one for every 1,000 people. These missionary teams would start by training hundreds of church planters and work towards the ultimate goal of a DAWN project in every nation of the former Soviet empire.

To highlight the crisis in Western missions, no society was able to redeploy teams to meet this incredible opening and opportunity. Still, Jay Weaver, Training Director in Budapest, reports that The Alliance has brought together 31 mission societies and 24 major churches in the U.S. as official partners. They have fielded 15 teams composed of new missionaries and a few who moved from West to East Europe and have another 50 missionaries at large. Together, these are functioning in 17 of the nations in the region.

Besides the foreign missionaries involved, there were now 35 nationals assisting in the training of church planters. Furthermore, the *DAWN 2000* book had been published in Romanian and two editions of Russian, the first DAWN congress was scheduled for Estonia in the Fall of 1996, and DAWN projects were at least in beginning stages in three other nations.

Nor has the project been without significant progress. Woody Phillips, who served as Field Director for The Alliance and has now replaced Dwight Smith as UWM president and as Executive Director for the Alliance, reported that as of mid-1995, 1,500 national church planters had been trained and 503 churches planted with 18,421 in regular attendance. Evidence that congregations will continue to be multiplied is found in the fact that 4,909 small groups have been established that are attracting about 105,355 in average attendance. It is projected that at least half of these will become full-fledged churches.

Don Crane, a Greater Europe missionary with 26 years experience in the region, has replaced Woody Phillips as Field Director in the Budapest office. "The Alliance is the most significant missionary cooperative effort ever to come about in Europe," he says. "These societies have come together with the same vision. They have even committed their personnel and financial resources to this network. This is unheard of!

"There have been other massive efforts, of course, but never bringing the mission societies together and never with such an in-depth strategy."

"In response to the tremendous openness to the gospel in this region," Smith said at the time, "evangelicals have rushed in with a variety of evangelistic resources that were immediately available. But the time has quickly come when in-depth and long-range strategies must also be employed to meet the real and felt needs of the Church of that region."

For Smith, as we saw in Chapter Two, "in-depth and long-range" strategies could only mean working towards the goal of filling all these nations with dynamic, evangelical congregations. There is no question about Woody Phillips carrying on with this vision.

"Missionaries can do many different, valuable ministries on the field," he has written, "but The Alliance is focused on just one thing: saturation church planting. On the wall of the Budapest office of The Alliance is a sign that reads, 'We have succeeded when churches are planted.'

"The measure of success is not the training of church planters but the actual formation of multiplying congregations. That result defines the true goal we share."

While "networking" and "partnering" have become oft-repeated buzz words in missions circles, The Alliance is making it happen. "There is a wider sense of ownership and commitment than ever before among participating agencies," says Don Byers of United World Mission. In fact, most of the 15 teams already functioning on the field are each composed of missionaries from several agencies.

"They have chosen the good of the Kingdom over the expansion of their own mission's work in that area," writes Phillips. "Together we own the goal of filling these republics with churches, and are able to think and plan strategically toward the fulfillment of that goal. They have seen and are enjoying the benefits of sharing gifts and ideas and resources so that the national Church can receive the greater good of combined ministry. This also serves as a model of unity for the national Church. And everyone is enjoying it!"

These field teams are served by Regional Resource Teams in Budapest and Moscow who provide training resources, materials, expertise, advice and overall coordination for the joint effort. There are also 12 Area Facilitators that represent eight different agencies. Phillips also says of these leaders that "They are doing a good job—getting virtually nothing from it for their own agencies and churches, but a great deal of satisfaction in serving the whole Body of Christ. The partnership works because these eleven people are committed to facilitating everyone else."

As I evaluate the history and progress of The Alliance, it seems to me that it is jreally just at the bottom of the curve, that a powerful foundation has been laid that will see the vision of 300,000 more churches become the driving force of all who work in this incredible region of the world.

United World Mission and The Alliance are dramatically proving that the Body of Christ can truly function as a body, even across organizational lines. As this type of cooperation continues to proliferate around the world, we have another sign of the revival we are in and another assurance that the discipling of all nations can be accomplished in our time.

A veteran missionary is reborn

Still another model representing a paradigm shift for Western missions was developed by Elmer Kilbourne, also a high-energy missionary who at the age of 75 is still vigorously pursuing his church-multiplication dream. We met him briefly in Chapter Seven.

He avoided one of the roadblocks encountered by the Alliance that can be described in the adage that "it takes a long time to turn a battleship around." Somewhat to the dismay of all of us involved in putting together the Alliance was how few mission societies could respond quickly to the incredible opportunities afforded by the collapse of communism and the proliferation of newly independent states carved out of the former Soviet Union. It was almost impossible in many cases to re-deploy missionaries to this newly-ripened harvest field. It was Japan after World War II all over again.

Kilbourne avoided all that bureaucratic hassle by simply hooking up with an organization that in effect would let him do what he wanted. The benefactor was Franklin Graham of Samaritan's Purse. What Kilbourne wanted was a free hand in bringing to bear the resources of the Korean Church and friends in the U.S. to establish 1,000 new congregations and 25 Bible schools in India and construct the buildings to house them.

With 40 years of missionary experience and the middle member of four generations of missionaries totaling 200 man-years of ministry in Korea, Kilbourne was no novice.

"On retirement in 1985," Kilbourne said in an interview with a group of us in Dawn Ministries, "I kept asking the Lord what I should do next. He kept saying 'India' and I kept saying, 'No.' After being in the best place in the world for 40 years, India was the last place I wanted to go."

Indeed, Korea had been good to him. He told us about the lay-training Bible schools that were the instrument of fantastic church growth. During his time in Korea, the Oriental Missionary Society (OMS) that his grandfather helped start in 1907 was holding these institutes four nights a week. Lay people would work eight to ten hours a day and then come study the Bible for three hours at night.

"With this approach, we saw over 1,500 churches started in Korea," he told us. Now God was calling him out of this fantastic harvest field and sending him to difficult, unresponsive, India.

"I tried to make a deal," he said. "'God, I'll give you

five years in India if you give me five years in China.'" He was reminding God that his original call had been to China where he spent one year with his brothers before the communists kicked them out.

"After ten years," he said, "I'm still waiting."

All his ministry in India is connected with the Evangelical Church of India (ECI) headed by Bishop Ezra Sargunam and affiliated with the OMS. In the last ten years he has seen ECI explode from about 150 churches and 30,000 members to about 850 churches with 300,000 members. That's 19 percent AAGR for churches and 26 percent AAGR for members! In India!

These 850 registered congregations, by the way, meet in reinforced concrete block buildings that seat about 200 on the floor. There are perhaps another 500 house churches scattered around the country.

"I'm excited that you are interested in India," Kilbourne told us. "I can't find many that are. There is not a place in India—and I've traveled from one end to the other—that I could not start a church. Furthermore, I would say 70 percent of our 300,000 converts are former Hindus. This is God's hour for India. We must take advantage of this."

Though India was not his first choice of ministry after mission policy forced his retirement, Kilbourne had spent many years instilling the vision of missions into his Korean students. This was the answer to his question of what a third-generation missionary should be doing in a country. The miraculous growth God was bringing to Korea was for the purpose of reaching the rest of Asia.

He began to see his responsibility, then, was to get the Church to understand that its ministry was not just in its community or the next town but across the whole world.

He found it was not an easy task in a nation where 4,000 years of Confucian ethic instilled the concept that nobody counts outside your family. Furthermore, Korea for centuries had been an isolated, hermitic kingdom. It wasn't until about 1979 that Koreans were able to travel abroad. Even then, American dollars were needed, a commodity that few possessed.

"I figured the best way to break this mentality," says Kilbourne, "was to get them to go see for themselves. So around 1980 I took a group of our top leaders on a two-week trip to India. None of us had any idea of what the country was like. It broke all our hearts.

"On return I asked them what God had been saying. They prayed and said they felt they should go back and build 100 churches in two years. That's what I like about Koreans—they're my kind of people. They get things done. Two years later almost to the day we went back and dedicated the 100th church the Koreans had built."

It was a few more years before Kilbourne retired and joined Samaritan's Purse at the invitation of Franklin Graham, its founder. "Franklin came to me and said he needed some help, but by then the Lord had given me a vision for India," Kilbourne said. "To scare Franklin off I gave him a four-page memorandum of agreement of what I was going to do: build 1,000 churches and 25 Bible schools in India."

Franklin didn't blink. Instead, he gave Kilbourne an open door and an open hand. "At my age and with the time I had left, I knew I could never reach these goals by working through the bureaucracy of a big organization," Kilbourne told us. "Franklin enabled me to do something that would have been totally impossible any other way."

Kilbourne made it clear that he is not talking about starting new congregations but about providing the buildings for the new congregations to meet in. The evangelism and church-planting work is supervised by Ezra Sargunam.

"Since I couldn't encompass everybody in India, I picked the organization that I knew best and worked with all my life. My total ministry is through ECI," says Kilbourne. "It is through OMS that ECI had a strong foundation. There is no way you can walk into a country and see this kind of thing happening without strong personnel. The ECI had them, but they were struggling with little finances. As soon as they were able to get a little seed money, this thing just took off.

"Ezra Sargunam is a man of unbelievable ability. I've worked with people in China and Asia all my life. I don't know of anybody that is a greater church planter. I don't start all those churches. I raise the funds for the buildings. He is the one who has developed that Church into a vital force in India."

Veteran missionary that he is, it is interesting to hear Kilbourne's perspective on church buildings.

"You don't need buildings in China," he told us. "When a pastor finishes Bible school or seminary in that nation, he goes out and rents a house for his family. The living room becomes the church. Chinese homes are built in a U shape. I've been in house churches with 600 to 800 people meeting in the courtyard.

"But this is not possible in India. The problem of building churches there is staggering. Before I will put up a building, the congregation must buy the land. This is very expensive, so the people have to sacrifice tremendously. In India there is no way for a congregation to become self supporting if they have to pay for a bigger facility.

"So in my opinion I believe we've got to construct church buildings if we are going to have rapid growth in India."

Approximately 300 of those 850 churches were funded by the Koreans at a cost of about $5,000 for a village church, $8,000 for a town church and $10,000 for a city church. In addition, Kilbourne has raised the funds for 10 Bible school facilities and plans to build three more each year for the next five years. He's also trying to build a seminary facility in Calcutta, a million dollar project.

"Koreans are still a major source of funds for these projects," he says. "I can do more in Korea in two days than six months in the United States. The Koreans are very generous in their giving. They are people who know the Lord and listen to him."

If Kilbourne believes in putting up solid buildings for congregations to meet in, he believes even more in solid training for the pastors who will lead these congregations. That's the reason for the 25 Bible schools he envisions.

A return to General George Patton

In my *DAWN 2000* book I referred to the approach of General George Patton during World War II. "I never tell my generals *how* to do something," he wrote in his autobiography. "I tell them *what* to do and they come up with all kinds of ingenious ways of getting it done."

Similarly, I'm not suggesting you should copy any one of the above models: starting a new society from scratch, totally remaking your current society, providing personnel and other resources for cooperative alliances or freeing yourself to work with the Church in one nation to multiply churches in another. The Lord might lead you to do one of these. On the other hand, reading about these models might stir your creative thinking to develop still other approaches that will bring about a paradigm shift from "general missionary work," as one person described his ministry, to the approach to saturation church planting that will work in your situation.

Still, there are some obvious things any Western mission society can do to enhance the cause of filling the earth with the knowledge of the glory of the Lord through saturation church planting efforts.

One, each mission society through prayer and analysis of data can set church-multiplication goals for their entire organization. This sometimes works best when the national counterpart in each nation sets its own goals. Added together, this becomes the international goal for the society. Other approaches can work as well.

Also in the *DAWN 2000* book, I wrote about the goals and plans of three societies in particular that had developed growth projects for their entire world-wide ministry. In checking back with these and other mission agencies, we found they had run into several snags.

Some had found it almost impossible, for example, to get accurate information on the number of churches and number of new churches planted from their denominational counterparts on the field. Record keeping and data gathering had not become a priority item.

The Southern Baptists were an exception to this. As of 1993, they were virtually on target in their "Bold Mission Thrust" project of increasing from 7,584 churches in 1976 to 75,000 by AD 2000 and seeing a similar ten-fold increase in members from 896,063 to nine million. The first 14 years of their program saw them running slightly behind their schedule, but growth rates of 16 percent in 1991 and 17 percent in 1992 brought them almost back in line with their projections.

While others were having problems with data gathering and goal setting, many reported they were constantly encouraging, inspiring and training their national denominations to keep up their zeal for an ever increasing multiplication of new congregations. With some success, I might add!

A natural follow-up to this is to help counterpart national denominations and missions to keep accurate records, gather annual data and set goals and carry out plans for church multiplication projects.

Two, Bible schools and seminaries continue to be an area where Western missionaries have a vital role and therefore still have considerable influence in many lands. By now, these schools should have long since modeled a burning zeal and developed vigorous training in the skills needed for saturation church planting and starting multiplying, church-planting churches.

The still flourishing One, One, One project of Chris Marantika mentioned in Chapter Seven continues to be a model of what can be done. His requirement that every student actually plant a church before graduation has already resulted in more than 700 hundred being started since 1979. These students also commit themselves to the vision of filling their nation with evangelical congregations. This approach should become standard practice for Bible and theological institutions around the world.

This training and zeal should also be part of the preparation for missionaries being sent from two-thirds world nations to the 10/40 window and other cross cultural endeavors. There has been much talk about the great number of such missionaries being sent, but I have heard little of what they are supposed to do when they get there. Unless they are armed with a vision of multiplying churches, they can easily fall into the trap of using familiar methodologies that produce little or no growth when other methods might produce a great harvest.

Three, it is time to take seriously the unity of the Body of Christ and the need for networking that we are all talking about. As this relates to a shift to a saturation church planting mentality and the completion of the Great Commission in a nation, Western mission societies can encourage and support national strategies of this nature. Whether they are sponsored by national evangelical fellowships, the AD2000 Movement, *ad hoc* committees or whether they use the name DAWN or any other for their project is not the point. It is the great strength that comes when the Body of Christ perceives itself as a body and functions as a body.

To establish and year after year maintain such a national initiative requires a considerable amount of effort and resources which Western societies can help provide both for their denominational counterparts as well as for the national strategy committee.

A beautiful expression of this comes from the mother DAWN project in the Philippines where "Leaders are no longer saying, 'We have 500 churches' (in our denomination) but, 'We have 35,000 churches' (in our nation)."

Mike Downey gave expression to this as well. "For 17 years," he said in our interview, "I have been asking why somebody doesn't bring coordination to the overall task of completing the Great Commission. We've had this command for two thousand years!

"But when I read your book in Korea, I said, 'Man, this is what I have been looking for for years. You've already done it.' We believe in the DAWN strategy. How can we help you facilitate that strategy?"

Though the challenge he feels from the Lord is to see those nine million churches planted just through his ministry "or die trying," he recognizes this will really happen only when the "20 percent of the Church that does 80 percent of the work" is committed to working together towards this goal. And in reality, his missionaries and short-term lay people are always working with and through local churches and denominations around the world.

This is the spirit and the cooperation needed to truly work effectively at making disciples of all nations in our time.

Neither Mike Downey and his Global Mission Fellowship nor Dawn Ministries nor the AD2000 and Beyond Movement nor the unreached peoples networks nor any other entity, of course, is going to do it all by themselves. Under the guidance and unifying ministry of the Holy Spirit, it will take the effort of all the key leaders of the Church and the people and structures they control and influence.

Even given such a paradigm shift by the whole missions community and the Church worldwide, we still need light on the task. How far have we come in saturating every nation and people group with evangelical congregations and what is the task that remains?

That is the subject for the final chapter.

Chapter 10

And then the end will come

'For the first time since the first century, the evangelization of the world is within our grasp.'

David Shibley[1]
Evangelical author

If a paradigm shift, a change in the way we look at and do things, is important for the small but still significant part Western missions play in completing the Great Commission, how much more so for the Church of the whole world.

For as Leighton Ford has written, "If our goal is the penetration of the whole world, then...we must aim at nothing less than the mobilization of the whole Church."[2]

How far has the whole Body come in filling the earth with the knowledge of the glory of the Lord with the presence of the incarnate Christ in every small community of mankind?

Ralph Winter of the US Center for World Mission and I have discussed this on occasion. Working backwards from an estimated 650 million true believers—or "Great Commission Christians" as researcher David Barrett calls them—in the world as of 1993, we concluded and agreed this meant about 4,300,000 congregations. We arrived at this by estimating an average of 60 adult, communicant members per church, and a rule-of-thumb 2.5 times that number comprising the total evangelical community including children and others who attend. That means 150 evangelicals per church divided into 650 million to get the 4,300,000 figure. If congregations are increasing by 4.5 percent AAGR, as Patrick Johnstone indicates,[3] this would mean 4,907,000 or close to five million churches by the end of 1996.

At a continued rate of just 4.5 percent AAGR, there would be about one "Great Commission church" for every 1,000 people on average in the world by the end of AD 2000. This is the goal we have been suggesting as a minimum to fill every nation and people group with congregations. This is the primary target for SCP.

Looking at the *average* of one church per 1,000 people in the world, of course, hides more than it reveals. For the 172 million unsaved people in the USA we could easily need 172,000 more congregations, despite the reality of 375,000 churches already here. Surely we need 30,000 congregations at least for the 30 million whose first language is other than English. Another 10,000 in the black community and 5,000 or more for the Hispanics. The list could go on and on.

Or take another look at the peoples of the Amazon basin that we wrote about in Chapter Two. Since there are about 17 million people in this vast region, our rule of thumb would suggest a need for 17,000 churches. Luke Huber, however, observed that great numbers of these people live in villages of around 50 people. Since he concluded a church is needed for *every* village, he estimated a need for 80,000 more congregations just in the river basin plus 20,000 more in other Portuguese-speaking communities.

Then we take a major leap into the world of unreached peoples with their many hundreds of millions still outside the range of a church in their village, neighborhood, culture and homogeneous unit.

The good news is that we have come a long way in

"churching" the nations of the world. The challenging news requiring an all-out effort by every member of Church and mission is that there are still millions of churches to be planted.

Anticipating exponential growth

In my opinion, however, the good news far outweighs the bad. Based on in-depth spot checks here and there, it is evident there are a lot more churches in the world than we are able to count or estimate, that they could be or soon will be increasing in number faster than current data indicates and that it is not going to take as long to fill unreached people groups with congregations as has been the situation in the "reached" nations of the world.

Concerning the last point, Nepal gives us a beautiful illustration. Before 1950, current Christian leaders there say there were no known believers in this Hindu kingdom. My friend Lok Mani Bhandari says that according to information he has received, there were 25 baptized believers in 1960, 25,000 by 1985 and more than 50,000 by 1991. When I spoke with him at Fuller Seminary where he was studying in 1994, he said that "Growth is so rapid that it is almost impossible to keep track. By now there are at least 100,000 believers but there could be as many as 150,000." His vision even before he heard of DAWN was to plant 16,000 churches throughout the Himalayas.

Back to the New Testament

Part of my optimism for the possibility of accelerated or even exponential growth stems from a growing trend to redefine "church" along more biblical lines. In Chapter Seven, for example, we quote John DeVries as saying that the 87,000 "Witnessing Prayer Cells" established in India in the first eight years of their Mission India project "...are full churches in every New Testament sense."

By this he means they consist of a gathered group of

disciples who meet regularly under the leadership of elders who perform the basic sacraments of baptism and the Lord's Supper. By this definition of "church" and with their strategy and rate of growth, it is not beyond reason that they could reach their goal of one such "church" for every 1,000 Indians—850,000 in all—in currently reached and unreached people groups within a ten-year period. And they're not the only ones multiplying churches in India by far!

Interest in this approach that might be called the cell-based church is growing worldwide, according to Carl F. George, Director of the Charles E. Fuller Institute of Evangelism and Church Growth, Pasadena, California.[4]

"It's a church with no more similarity with a program-based, traditional church than a caterpillar has with a butterfly," George said in a recent issue of *Cell Church Magazine.* "In Christian communities from Orthodox to Anabaptist, Pentecostal to Lutheran, the notion of a cell-driven church is completely reorienting our understanding of the nature of ministry."

Ralph W. Neighbour, Jr., founder and president of Touch Outreach Ministries, Houston, Texas, and a former professor of church planting, has a similar viewpoint. "The traditional church worldwide is slowly being replaced by an act of God," he said in his book *Where Do People Go From Here?* "Developments taking place today are as powerful as the upheaval in 1517 during the time of Martin Luther."

A growing cell-church movement

One third-world model of the cell-based church is Faith Community Baptist Church (FCBC) in Singapore. Senior pastor Lawrence Khong, a relatively new convert to the idea, hosted The Second International Conference of Cell Group Churches in March, 1993.

"There needs to be a fundamental change in the structure of the church," he told the 800 delegates from 13 countries. "The church needs to return to what are its biblical roots—the cell penetrating the community."

A year after Khong began FCBC in 1987, the church had 600 members and no cells. By 1993, however, it had more than 4,000 members in over 400 cell groups. Their goal was to double this in the next year and to have a cell church in every one of Singapore's 5,000 apartment buildings by AD 2000.

The cell, according to Khong and other cell church advocates, is not just a small group. It is, they say, the church—a place for worship, ministry, prayer, encouragement and edification. The cell, the smallest unit in the church body, is a structure where eight to 15 believers minister to one another and work together to reach the lost. Through personal evangelism, the cell is expected to grow and multiply, usually within six months to a year. The senior pastor's main responsibilities are leading and edifying the entire congregation, primarily through the Sunday service, and training leaders who will train others.

"There will always be people who think their Christian life is just going to a meeting and, 'As long as I've gone to church and am not really doing bad things, I'm okay,'" Khong said at the 1993 conference.

"But we think that every Christian is responsible to minister and to share the gospel" he said. "In the cell, each member is challenged about his attitudes and lifestyle. He is also surrounded by a community where he can find care, love, healing, edification and encouragement. The world is attracted to that."

Because proselytizing is restricted in Singapore, many churches—Evangelical Free, Methodist, Anglican, Baptist, to name a few—are turning to the cell group structure as an effective, low-key model for reaching the lost.

Worldwide, most cell group churches support and send their own missionaries, Khong said. "Many missionaries who go out to the field to plant a church have never pastored one before," according to Khong. "But in the cell group concept, our missionaries have gone through our training program and have learned to pastor a cell. District pastors often pastor as many as 1,000 members, so when they go out as missionaries, they have hands-on experience."

FCBC also ministers to hard-to-reach non-believers through Touch Community Services, which includes child and family care, welfare services, legal aid, diabetes support, counseling and work with the disabled.

Other mega-churches with this cell orientation include Yoido Full Gospel Church in Korea with 600,000 members; Mana Ingreja Cristo in Lisbon, Portugal, with 75,000 members; Eglise Portestante Baptiste Oeurvreset Mission in Abidjan, Cote d'Ivoire, with 30,000 members; and Hope of Bangkok Church, Bangkok, Thailand, with 10,000 members. As we saw in Chapter Three, much of the accelerated rate of church planting in England is through house churches, and there is even a small but rapidly growing house church movement developing in the U.S.

This approach to saturation church planting might be especially appropriate in "churching" the unreached people groups of the world, for it lends itself very much to an underground or "unofficial" movement such as we have seen in China and other places. There is even one major Islamic nation where there is an actual goal and plan being implemented to fill it with one "church" for every 1,000 Muslims. The "churches" consist of small groups that are very contextualized. They don't call these groups "churches" nor do they identify with the visible evangelical movement in the country. Some argue the validity of this approach, but I for one will not say the Holy Spirit can not use this means to disciple this huge unreached people.

It is such rethinking and reformulating of what we mean by "church" that could greatly accelerate reaching the goal of a congregation for every small community of people on the face of the earth in our time.

A strategy for the end of the age

Is this DAWN/SCP idea catching on? Is this what God wants to happen in our time? Is this what he is saying to his prophets and apostles of today? Is it a strategy of his for the end of the age, however close or distant that end might be?

There does seem to be a growing momentum to the movement. The DAWN idea was first introduced to the Church of a nation in the Philippines in 1974. It was ten years before the Church in Guatemala became the second nation to hold a national congress and set a national goal. In these years, DAWN-type projects were also developing in Indonesia and Ghana.

So there were four such national projects underway in 1985 when Dawn Ministries was formed. Eleven years later, more than 100 nations representing over 85 percent of the world's population have a DAWN or DAWN-type project in motion.[5] More than 30 of these projects have passed the national congress and goal setting phase with a total of close to three million new churches projected. Each year, several more nations hold their first DAWN congress, and many have their second or third. The Philippine Church will soon hold its sixth. With the current rate of expansion, we expect the number of nations with an SCP/DAWN project underway will reach 145 covering more than 96 percent of the world's population by the end of 1998.

Since these projects are all developed, predominently funded and totally carried out by national leaders, we can conclude they really believe in what they are doing.

Furthermore, we counted over 65 mission and parachurch organizations participating in DAWN projects in just three nations we researched. These included such well-known ministries as Campus Crusade for Christ, The Bible League, Every Home for Christ, OC International, Greater

Europe Mission and five dozen others.

Perhaps of even greater significance is that scores of denominations including virtually all the major ones are participating in DAWN projects within individual countries. This network covering whole nations and some whole regions of the world is well beyond the talking stage and deeply into functioning as the Body of Christ in actually building his kingdom.

World movements embrace DAWN

Integration at the highest levels of international cooperation in world evangelization is also now an accomplished fact.

The Lausanne Committee for World Evangelization became the first to acknowledge the DAWN strategy. This is the structure backed by the Billy Graham Association that hosted major congresses on world evangelization in 1974 (Lausanne, Switzerland) and 1989 (Manila, Philippines) and many other regional and topical conferences.

Tom Houston, who served as Lausanne Committee International Director for a number of years, made the comment before a small group of international leaders that DAWN "is one of the great movements of our time." He told us on another occasion that the Lausanne Committee several years ago had endorsed the DAWN strategy in lieu of developing their own national projects.

Furthermore, when Agustin (Jun) Vencer, Jr., became International Director of the World Evangelical Fellowship (WEF) in 1992, he began reshaping its vision along the lines of the "DAWN 2000" project he had led for many years in the Philippines. In 1993, therefore, the WEF Board of Directors changed their purpose statement to include the goal of establishing a saturation church planting project in every one of its 114 national fellowships that represent 150 million believers.

Then, in 1994, we signed a Mutual Assistance Agreement statement with WEF providing for Dawn Ministries to serve as their evangelism and church planting arm. "For our part," Vencer said at the time, "we will encourage all our affiliates to commit themselves to a national project along the lines of the DAWN strategy, and we will encourage them to seek your help."

A third major world movement for world evangelization that has also fully embraced the SCP/DAWN vision burst on the scene in 1989 and reached a high point with the Global Consultation on World Evangelization (GCOWE) in 1995. Gathering for this major event were about 4,000 delegates from 186 countries in Seoul, Korea, May 17-26.

This was the AD2000 and Beyond Movement that is flying under the banner of "A Church for Every People and the Gospel for Every Person by the Year 2000."

Though it ultimately focused its attention primarily on the unreached peoples of the world, virtually every facet of its component parts—called tracks—had a strong SCP element.

Peter Wagner, who heads the AD2000 Prayer Track, says, "I take the AD2000 slogan to mean 'A local church within easy access of every person in every country and people group. The DAWN idea of one congregation for every 500 to 1,000 people of every class, kind and condition of mankind sounds about right to me.'

"Actually," he goes on to say, "our purpose in the Prayer Track is to support the saturation church planting vision. Most other AD2000 tracks are also a means to the end of a vast multiplication of new churches in nations and people groups. They are not ends in themselves."

The Cities Resource Network Track states in part that "To fulfill the Great Commission, we must see Christ become incarnate in vital, witnessing (in word and deed) congregations, culturally and geographically accessible to every community in every city."[6]

The end result of the Saturation *Evangelism* Track is "...to ensure that a leadership training opportunity is available to train the leaders for the groups of new converts that will be reached."[7] What are "groups of new converts" under "leaders" that have been "trained" if they are not nascent churches?

Even the Unreached Peoples Track stated that their end goal is "...that holistic mission-minded church-planting movements may emerge...."[8]

For about five years I headed the SCP Track along with Chris Marantika who developed the One, One, One project in Indonesia. It is not surprising, then, that we wrote part of our statement for the *AD2000 Handbook* to read:

> To complete the Great Commission, it is necessary not only to enter each nation (the primary missionary task) but to make a disciple of each nation (country, people group, city, etc.). A growing number of leaders around the world agree this happens best when we are engaged in seeing Christ become incarnate in the life of a vital, witnessing congregation among every group of 500 to 1,000 people of every class, kind and condition of mankind.[9]

In listing the basic assumptions of the national AD2000 initiatives, the *AD2000 Handbook* states that the objective of many national plans is "Seeking to establish a church-planting movement in every village and every colony of every town and city so that Christ can be incarnated through His Body within access of every person on earth."[10]

This became an even stronger focus when the first follow-up meeting of AD2000 after GCOWE was held in Colorado Springs November 28 to December 2, 1995. This gathering for 262 international leaders from 77 nations was referred to as "The Launch." Being "launched" was the Joshua Project, a plan for mobilizing resources for the unreached peoples of the 10/40 window, and the AD2000 National Initiative Movement, a design for developing national strategies in countries all over the world.

My enthusiasm for the Joshua Project as presented was that it aimed at establishing church-planting movements in each of the 2,085 unreached people groups with a population of at least 10,000. This would greatly enhance the possibility of fanning the flames of these efforts into full-scale saturation-church-planting projects, moving them from pioneer mission efforts to making disciples of these peoples or nations.

My joy increased when a paper describing the AD2000 National Initiatives was presented by its authors Ross Campbell and Bob Waymire. In this document, SCP had been dropped as a separate track and instead was lodged at the peak or end result to be aimed at in each country. The document clearly stated that "Ultimately, the goal is to see a gathering of Bible-believing Christians within practical and cultural distance of every person in every class and kind of people, penetrating every neighborhood with the transforming love, care, truth and power of Jesus Christ."[11]

It went on to list the nine components of a National AD2000 Initiative, components that for 20 years had been the backbone of the DAWN strategy.

What is God trying to say?

So with the AD2000 and Beyond Movement at the end of 1995 fully embracing what is in effect the DAWN strategy, we now had all three major international evangelical bodies concerned for world evangelization expressing solidarity and unanimity in a strategy for the discipling of nations. Each was committed to filling all countries and "nations"—i.e., people groups—with the presence of the risen Christ in the form of biblical congregations.

I have taken the time to explain all this simply because of what I believe is the enormous significance of this convergence. With all three international structures endorsing the DAWN vision, it was now "politically" possible for all regional and national fellowships to cooperate in strategies without the sometimes endless deliberations of whose strategy to embrace.

Now Church leaders within any nation, whether they identified more closely with Lausanne, WEF, AD2000 or even Dawn Ministries, could develop a DAWN-type strategy and know they had the backing and endorsement of their international affiliate. Now any spirit of competition could be knocked in the head, since all were in agreement as to the nature of the national strategy they should pursue. Now the enormous power that results from the unity of the Body of Christ could be unleashed.

As had already happened many times on the national level, now the Body of Christ at the international level was beginning to perceive itself as a body and to function as a body. Could it be that this emerging consensus on a workable and proven strategy for making disciples of all nations is another sign of the world revival we are in?

With the enthusiastic endorsement and involvement of all the above people and structures, we can now ask the same rhetorical question that launched the AD2000 Movement: "Is God Trying to Tell Us Something?"[12]

If every church were like this!

If he is, it wouldn't take long to complete the task if every pastor and Christian worker in the world had the vision of Pastor Ambe in the Philippines. Since the DAWN strategy emerged in the Philippines more than 20 years ago, it is only fitting that I begin to wrap up this final chapter with this Filipino's story of his Bankerohan Alliance Church.

Pastor Ambe pretty much sums up the vision of DAWN with this simple statement: "Our strategy is to multiply churches, our chief method is the evangelistic home Bible study group but our power is in prayer."

Here's what this approach produced in just one 19-

month period: The church membership increased 1,500 percent from 80 members to 1,300. His small mother church planted 35 new congregations, each with a full-time pastor and an average of 35 members. His congregation has set its sights on planting a total of 300 new churches by the end of AD 2000.

Furthermore, they now have dreams of sending ten missionaries to Indonesia to multiply churches there. "It is not right that we look at the needs of our own people without also seeing the needs of other peoples," he says.

Pastor Ambe discounts his own role in all this and gives credit to the prayer emphasis of his people. He reports that at any hour of the day from 6:00 a.m. to 8:00 p.m. there are at least four groups praying in different locations. An average of 50 participants also attend the 6:00 a.m. to 12:00 midnight prayer sessions every Wednesday.

"This is what has produced our church-planting effort," says Ambe. He also credits the Outreach Bible Study method as being the most effective in planting new congregations.

Ambe gets his church-planting workers from the pool of Alliance pastors in Davao—the city where he is located—and from the local Davao Alliance Bible College. Laymen and women from his church are also involved in helping with preaching, teaching, Sunday School, conducting children's outreaches, visitation and counseling.

In the early days of the program, new churches were started by "hiving off" members who lived in areas remote from the mother church. This is why the mother church has remained at 80 members. "We continually add new members, but we hive them off as fast as we get them," Ambe says.

The full-time workers who lead church planting efforts are financed through setting aside a fixed amount from the mother church annual budget and also from believers outside the local church who want to help. He also works in partnership with other churches who contribute an agreed amount. "If they make the majority effort," says Ambe, "we are willing to let the church belong to their denomination."

In the rural areas, much of the support for new churches comes from livelihood projects. Members who have farms are challenged to plant fast-yielding crops such as peanuts and corn with the proceeds going to the new church. "Seedlings are provided by the mother church," explains Ambe. "The landowner donates his time and efforts until the crop is harvested."

Salaries for pastors of the new churches are adjusted according to the annual increase of the cost of living and according to the local economy. They range from about $75 a month in the cities to as low as $20 in rural areas.

Pastor Ambe has caught the vision and is doing more than his share to help the Christian and Missionary Alliance Churches of the Philippines (CAMACOP) reach their national goal of 10,000 churches and one million members by AD 2000.

He is also providing an excellent example for local churches all over the country and, through this book, all over the world. He certainly has put all the ingredients together: A *big* vision and the right *kind* of vision. Challenging goals. A kingdom mentality of working in cooperation with other congregations. In-depth prayer backing. Wise use of a cell-church strategy. Involvement of lay people and effective training for pastors. A financial structure that is indefinitely reproducible. A plan to send missionaries to a 10/40 window country.

It is the dream and prayer of leaders in every DAWN project to have every pastor and Church leader catch this vision. For if every Christian worker in the world had a vision like his, though modified to fit the economic and cultural realities of his or her situation, it wouldn't be long before we would hear that final trumpet blast calling us up to meet with the Lord in the air. With the worldwide Body of Christ united on an SCP strategy like this, we could have this whole task wrapped up well before AD 2010.

Looking to the year 2010

That is why I wrote *DAWN 2000: 7 Million Churches to Go*. It was to enhance the possibility that the Church of every nation could be mobilized to speed the process of seeing all this fulfilled. But should the Lord tarry beyond the end of this century, our responsibility continues.

That is also why I believe, as good stewards of the responsibility that has been given us, we ought to begin now thinking about the decade following the year 2000. The year 2010, of course, is no more a magic date than AD 2000, nor the year 2009 that Rev. Barton saw as the last possible date mentioned in the Bible.

AD 2010 is simply another convenient target for the next phase of world evangelization that the Church can rally around, set its goals for, and make and implement its next set of plans for. In fact, in the August, 1994, issue of our *DAWN Report* Magazine, I wrote an item entitled "Do we have AD 2000 backwards?"

> ...perhaps we *have* been putting too much emphasis on this date as a time when the task could be *completed*. I'm wondering if we should not think of AD 2000 as a time to be fully prepared to *begin* a massive, comprehensive effort towards world evangelization in the following decades.
>
> If by the year 2000 the Church were mobilized in every nation with the needed experience and workable plan to see a congregation planted within easy access both culturally and physically of every person—and were sending missionaries to help with that task in countries where most needed—*then* perhaps we could talk realistically about completing the Great Commission.

Naturally, I vigorously support the massive spread of the gospel message through every means the Lord makes available and I am profoundly concerned that movements to Christ are begun among all who have yet to see a viable Christian Church in their midst. These crucial aspects of the Great Commission must be pursued by all with the gifting and calling to do so.

I am concerned, however, that whether or not the gospel has been made somehow available to every person and the Church has taken root in every soil by the year 2000 that there will be a massive let-down after that date. If we don't reach the goal of "A Church for every people and the Gospel for every person", there will be discouragement. If we make it, the tendency will be to relax in our efforts. But until the Lord returns, the job is not done. There is the necessity to continue to press forward to see that the glory of the Lord is resplendent in the midst of every small community of mankind as long as the Church exists.

It would be more than fantastic if the Lord should return during the year 2000—or before! Should that not happen, however, good stewardship requires of us that we be found diligently working in the harvest field until the very last moment.

The strategy we suggest for the end of the age until the Lord returns is that every ministry of the Church and missions be aimed at saturation church planting, at filling every nation and people group with cells of believers that are filled with the Spirit and emulate the life of Jesus Christ. This is the big picture we must embrace. This is what the power of the emerging world revival makes possible. This is what can and must be done in our time. This is what I believe the Lord requires of us as we live and minister in the time of the end, as we look to the close of the age.

The profound nature of this strategy, I believe, is summed up in Paul's letter to the Colossians (1:28):

> We proclaim him, admonishing and teaching

everyone with all wisdom, so that we may present everyone perfect in Christ.

We want to "proclaim" the gospel to *everyone* both in reached and unreached areas. In our time, this calls for a determined effort in taking the gospel to every still unreached people group as well as a comprehensive spreading of the gospel by every means the Lord makes available to all peoples everywhere.

But, according to this verse, we also want to admonish and teach *everyone* to the end that *each* may be presented *perfect* in Christ. This can only happen when new believers are gathered in a teaching, growing, worshipping, discipling environment: that is, in a church. And only when there are churches *everywhere* in the nations and people groups of the world can such a setting be made available to *everyone*!

This is the essence of the DAWN/Saturation Church Planting concept and the strategy we suggest for working most directly at completing the Great Commission in our time.

The good news, the inspiring news, is that more and more of God's choice servants around the world are not only catching this vision but giving their lives to it and thereby hastening the day when the task will be accomplished. Most assuredly, our abiding hope is that one day the last convert will be made, the last church planted.

"...and then the end will come."

---

[1] David Shibley, *A Force in the Earth* (Creation House, Lake Mary, FL, 1989) p. 16-17.

[2] Leighton Ford, *The Christian Persuader* (Minneapolis, World Wide Publications, 1988), p.45.

[3] Patrick Johnstone, *Operation World* (Grand Rapids, MI: Zondervan Publishing House, 1993), p.26.

[4] Material in this section including the statistics on large, cell group-based churches is taken from "*Pulse*," June 25, 1993 and used with permission.

[5] Information about DAWN projects around the world can be obtained by writing to Dawn Ministries.

[6] Luis Bush, Editor, *AD2000 And Beyond Handbook* (Colorado Springs, CO: AD2000 And Beyond Movement, Third Edition, 1993), p.23.

[7] Ibid., p.25.

[8] Ibid., p.22.

[9] Ibid., p.21.

[10] Ibid., p 5.

[11] Ross Campbell, Robert Waymire, "National AD2000 Initiative Working Document."

[12] In the late 1980's Thomas Wang, then International Director of the Lausanne Committee for World Evangelization, began to note there were a number of movements focused on plans and strategies, DAWN among them, for world evangelization. This led to a magazine article with the title, "By the Year 2000: Is God trying to tell us something?" The significant interest aroused by this question led to the first consultation on world evangelization by AD 2000 held in Singapore in 1989.

How can we help?

Dawn Ministries was founded, we believe, under the direct leading of the Lord to promote the vision of Saturation Church Planting (SCP) and to fan the flames of the DAWN Movement for world evangelization and the completion of the Great Commission in our time.

As the Lord provides for our financial needs, our nine missionaries travel to and communicate with national leaders anywhere in the world. They are eager to share the vision, explain the process, train researchers, give counsel to leaders and help in any other way possible.

We want to make it clear, however, that we take no authority over any national project. DAWN-type projects are owned and developed by the Church of a nation and by national leaders who are called by God to mobilize the national Churches for the discipling of their nations.

We exist only to help where our assistance is requested.

Dawn Ministries also provides useful literature that keeps the reader abreast of what God is doing through DAWN projects around the world and for learning more about what makes DAWN work.

DAWN REPORT, our 16-page quarterly magazine that provides this information, is sent free of charge to all who request it.

For further information about the services and ministries of Dawn Ministries or information about DAWN projects in individual nations, write:

Dawn Ministries
7899 Lexington Drive #200-B
Colorado Springs, CO 80920
U.S.A.
Phone: (719) 548 7460
Fax: (719) 548-7475
CompuServe address: 71102,2745

Index

OTHER MISSION BOOKS FROM WILLIAM CAREY LIBRARY

For a complete catalog write:
William Carey Library
P. O. Box 40129
Pasadena, CA 91114

THE BIBLE IN CROSS-CULTURAL PERSPECTIVE, by Jacob A. Loewen, 1997, paperback, 298 pages.
This book is about discovering more of the message of the Bible than we see through the eyes of our own culture. An excellent aid to translators and missionaries communicating the message of Christ.

COMMUNICATING CHRIST IN ANIMISTIC CONTEXTS, by Gailyn Van Rheenen, 1996, paperback, 344 pages.
Communicating Christ in Animistic Contexts shows that animistic beliefs are ubiquitous today, whether in New Age mysticism, horoscope occultism, Haitian voodooism, Chinese ancestor veneration, or Japanese Shintoism. Gailyn Van Rheenen presents a rigorous biblical, theological, and anthropological foundation for ministering in animistic contexts overseas or next door.

CULTURE AND HUMAN VALUES: Christian Intervention in Anthropological Perspective, by Jacob A. Leowen, 1975, paperback, 443 pages.
As an anthropologist, Dr. Loewen is particularly sensitive to the human and personal factors in personal and group behavior, and he is especially competent in describing some of the spiritual dimensions in the development of indigenous leadership.

CRISIS AND HOPE IN LATIN AMERICA: An Evangelical Perspective (Revised Edition), by Emilio Antonio Nunez C. and William David Taylor, 1996, paperback, 544 pages.
Nunez and Taylor expand their earlier work on Latin America. This revision incorporates an insightful essay by Peruvian missiologist Samuel Escobar, an updated section by Nunez and Taylor, and an expanded annotated bibliography.

DAWN 2000: Seven Million Churches to Go. The Personal Story of the DAWN Strategy by James Montgomery 1989, paperback, 24 pages.
Of all the strategies to evangelize the world, the concept of national-level collaboration is probably the most crucial and essential. This

book by a competent writer is a beautiful, personal unfolding of what is now a movement at work in twenty-six nations. You will not be able to put it down!

MEDIA IN CHURCH AND MISSION: Communicating the Gospel, by Viggo Sogaard, 1993, paperback, 304 pages.
A readable and practical synthesis of what has been learned through the new wave of thinking about communications.

MESSAGE AND MISSION: The Communication of the Christian Faith (Revised), by Eugene A. Nida, 1990, paperback, 300 pages.
Sharing the Christian life and truth is far more than using words and forms congenial to us, but strange and perhaps threatening in another culture. This book not only points the way to true communication but is foundational in this field.

PERSPECTIVES ON THE WORLD CHRISTIAN MOVEMENT: A Reader (Revised Edition), Ralph D. Winter and Steven C. Hawthorne, editors, 1992, paperback, 944 pages.
This text was designed to be the missionary platform of essential knowledge for all serious Christians who have only a secular education. Used as a basis for mission courses for fifteen years.

A PEOPLE FOR HIS NAME: A Church-Based Missions Strategy by Paul A. Beals, 1994, paperback, 260 pages.
A masterful overview of the roles of local churches, mission boards, missionaries and theological schools in the biblical fulfillment of the Great Commission.

RESEARCH IN CHURCH AND MISSIONS, by Viggo Søgaard, 1996, paperback, 280 pages.
A very useful instructional base for both the student learning the fundamentals of communication research and for the administrator of a research project. A base of communication theory sets the stage for the research methods in this book. Søgaard's worldwide consulting experience in communication research puts under one cover why and how systematic research methods and skills should be and could be used to improve effectiveness of Christian ministries.

ST. LUKE'S MISSIOLOGY: A Cross-Cultural Challenge, by Harold Dollar, 1996, paperback, 198 pages.
An exemplary integrative study with missiological conclusions that are weighty because they are firmly anchored in careful, multi-dimensional biblical scholarship.